PAINTING
OF THE
HIGH RENAISSANCE
IN
ROME AND FLORENCE

VOLUME II

PAINTING
OF THE
HIGH RENAISSANCE
IN
ROME AND FLORENCE

S. J. FREEDBERG

HARVARD UNIVERSITY PRESS

CAMBRIDGE, MASSACHUSETTS

1961

Distributed in Great Britain by Oxford University Press, London

Publication of these volumes has been aided by grants from the
Bollingen Foundation and from the Ford Foundation

Typography by Burton J. Jones

❋

Volume I printed in the U.S.A. by Harvard University Printing Office, Cambridge

❋

Volume II printed in England by W. S. Cowell Ltd., 8 Butter Market, Ipswich

❋

Bound by Stanhope Bindery, Boston

Library of Congress Catalog Card Number 61–7390

ILLUSTRATIONS

I

INTRODUCTION
THE GENESIS OF HIGH RENAISSANCE CLASSICAL STYLE

95. RIPANDA *Consul and Lictors*, Rome, Palazzo dei Conservatori. Photo Fototeca di Architettura e Topografia dell'Italia Antica, Rome
96. SODOMA *Central Octagon of the Stanza della Segnatura*, Rome, Vatican. Photo Alinari

III

THE MATURITY OF THE CLASSICAL STYLE IN ROME
(*c*. 1508–*c*. 1514)

97. MICHELANGELO *The Sistine Ceiling*, Rome, Vatican, Sistine Chapel. Photo Anderson
98. MICHELANGELO *The Sistine Ceiling* (central bays). Photo Archivio Fotografico delle Gallerie e Musei Vaticani
99. MICHELANGELO *Preliminary Plan for Sistine Ceiling*, London, British Museum. Photo museum. Courtesy of the Trustees of the British Museum
100. MICHELANGELO *Preliminary Plan for Sistine Ceiling*, Detroit, Institute of Arts. Photo museum. Courtesy of the Institute of Arts, Detroit
101. MICHELANGELO *Bronze-colored Nudes in the Spandrels*, Sistine Ceiling. Photo Archivio Fotografico delle Gallerie e Musei Vaticani
102. MICHELANGELO *Bronze-colored Nudes in the Spandrels*, Sistine Ceiling. Photo Archivio Fotografico delle Gallerie e Musei Vaticani
103. MICHELANGELO *The Flood*, Sistine Ceiling. Photo Archivio Fotografico delle Gallerie e Musei Vaticani
104. MICHELANGELO *Sacrifice of Noah*, Sistine Ceiling. Photo Anderson
105. MICHELANGELO *Drunkenness of Noah*, Sistine Ceiling. Photo Anderson
106. MICHELANGELO *Delphic Sibyl*, Sistine Ceiling. Photo Anderson
107. MICHELANGELO *Prophet Joel*, Sistine Ceiling. Photo Archivio Fotografico delle Gallerie e Musei Vaticani
108. MICHELANGELO *Prophet Zachary*, Sistine Ceiling. Photo Anderson
109. MICHELANGELO *Erithrean Sibyl*, Sistine Ceiling. Photo Anderson
110. MICHELANGELO *Prophet Isaiah*, Sistine Ceiling. Photo Anderson
111. MICHELANGELO *Ignudi around the Drunkennesss of Noah*, Sistine Ceiling. Photo Alinari
112. MICHELANGELO *Ignudo above Prophet Joel*, Sistine Ceiling. Photo Anderson
113. MICHELANGELO *Ignudo above Prophet Joel*, Sistine Ceiling. Photo Anderson
114. MICHELANGELO *Ignudi around Sacrifice of Noah*, Sistine Ceiling. Photo Alinari
115. MICHELANGELO *Ignudo above Prophet Isaiah*, Sistine Ceiling. Photo Anderson
116. MICHELANGELO *Ignudo above Prophet Isaiah*, Sistine Ceiling. Photo Anderson

140. MICHELANGELO *David and Goliath*, Sistine Ceiling. Photo Anderson
141. MICHELANGELO *Judith and Holofernes*, Sistine Ceiling. Photo Anderson
142. MICHELANGELO *The Hanging of Haman*, Sistine Ceiling. Photo Anderson
143. MICHELANGELO *The Brazen Serpent*, Sistine Ceiling. Photo Anderson
144. MICHELANGELO *Ancestors of Christ*, Sistine Ceiling, severies. Photo Anderson
145. MICHELANGELO *Ancestors of Christ*, Sistine Ceiling, severies. Photo Anderson
146. MICHELANGELO *Ancestors of Christ*, Sistine Ceiling, lunettes. Photo Alinari
147. MICHELANGELO *Ancestors of Christ*, Sistine Ceiling, lunettes. Photo Alinari
148. MICHELANGELO *Ancestors of Christ*, Sistine Ceiling. Photo Anderson
149. RAPHAEL *Stanza della Segnatura*, Rome, Vatican. Photo Gabinetto Fotografico Nazionale, Rome
150. RAPHAEL *Stanza della Segnatura*. Photo Alinari
151. RAPHAEL [and Sodoma] *Ceiling of the Stanza della Segnatura*. Photo Anderson
152. RAPHAEL *Poetry*, Stanza della Segnatura, ceiling. Photo Archivio Fotografico delle Gallerie e Musei Vaticani
153. RAPHAEL *Justice*, Stanza della Segnatura, ceiling. Photo Archivio Fotografico delle Gallerie e Musei Vaticani
154. RAPHAEL *The Flaying of Marsyas*, Stanza della Segnatura, ceiling. Photo Anderson
155. RAPHAEL *The Judgment of Solomon*, Stanza della Segnatura, ceiling. Photo Anderson
156. RAPHAEL *Disputà*, Stanza della Segnatura. Photo Anderson
157. RAPHAEL *Disputà* (detail). Photo Anderson
158. RAPHAEL *Disputà* (detail). Photo Anderson
159. RAPHAEL *Parnassus*, Stanza della Segnatura. Photo Archivio Fotografico delle Gallerie e Musei Vaticani
160. RAPHAEL *Parnassus* (detail), *Apollo and Muses*. Photo Anderson
161. RAPHAEL *Parnassus* (detail), *Sappho and Other Poets*. Photo Anderson
162. RAPHAEL *Parnassus* (detail), *Modern Poets*. Photo Archivio Fotografico delle Gallerie e Musei Vaticani
163. RAPHAEL *School of Athens*, Stanza della Segnatura. Photo Archivio Fotografico delle Gallerie e Musei Vaticani
164. RAPHAEL *School of Athens* (detail), *Plato and Aristotle*. Photo Achivio Fotografico delle Gallerie e Musei Vaticani
165. RAPHAEL *School of Athens* (detail), *Pythagorean Group*. Photo Archivio Fotografico delle Gallerie e Musei Vaticani
166. RAPHAEL *School of Athens* (detail), *Euclidian Group*. Photo Archivio Fotografico delle Gallerie e Musei Vaticani

243. RAPHAEL *St. Cecilia Altar* (detail). Photo Edizioni Cartovendita, Bologna

244. RAPHAEL *Tommaso Inghirami* ("Il Fedra"), Boston, Isabella Stewart Gardner Museum. Photo museum

245. RAPHAEL ASSISTANT *Tommaso Inghirami*, Florence, Pitti. Photo Anderson

246. RAPHAEL [or assistant] *Giuliano de' Medici*, New York, Metropolitan Museum. Photo museum. Courtesy of the Metropolitan Museum of Art

247. RAPHAEL *La Donna Velata*, Florence, Pitti. Photo Sopr. alle Gallerie, Florence

248. RAPHAEL *Madonna della Sedia*, Florence, Pitti. Photo Sopr. alle Gallerie, Florence

249. RAPHAEL *Madonna della Sedia* (detail). Photo Alinari

250. LEONARDO [and assistant?] *St. John Baptist*, Paris, Louvre. Photo Alinari

251. LEONARDO *Cataclysm*, Windsor, Royal Library. Photo Royal Library. Copyright reserved

IV

THE MATURATION OF CLASSICAL STYLE IN FLORENCE
(*c.* 1508–*c.* 1514)

252. FRA BARTOLOMMEO *Holy Family*, London, National Gallery 3914. Photo museum. Reproduced by courtesy of the Trustees, The National Gallery, London

253. FRA BARTOLOMMEO *God the Father with Sts. Mary Magdalen and Catherine of Siena*, Lucca, Pinacoteca. Photo Alinari

254. FRA BARTOLOMMEO [with Albertinelli] *Madonna with Six Saints*, Florence, S. Marco. Photo Alinari

255. FRA BARTOLOMMEO *Madonna with Sts. Stephen and John Baptist*, Lucca, Cathedral. Photo Alinari

256. ALBERTINELLI *Madonna with Four Saints*, Florence, Academy. Photo Alinari

257. ALBERTINELLI *Trinity*, Florence, Academy. Photo Sopr. alle Gallerie, Florence

258. ALBERTINELLI *Study for a Trinity*, Florence, Uffizi. Photo Sopr. alle Gallerie, Florence

259. ALBERTINELLI *Annunciation*, Florence, Academy. Photo Alinari

260. FRA BARTOLOMMEO *Marriage of St. Catherine*, Paris, Louvre. Photo Alinari

261. FRA BARTOLOMMEO [with Albertinelli] *Virgin in Glory with Saints*, Besançon, Cathedral. Photo Bulloz, Paris

262. ALBERTINELLI *Coronation of the Virgin* (fragment; former crown-piece of 261), Stuttgart, Gallery. Photo museum

263. FRA BARTOLOMMEO *St. Anne Altar*, Florence, Museo di S. Marco. Photo Sopr. alle Gallerie, Florence

264. FRA BARTOLOMMEO [with assistants] *The Marriage of St. Catherine* (the *Pitti Pala*), Florence, Academy. Photo Alinari

265. FRA BARTOLOMMEO [with Raphael] *St. Peter*, Rome, Vatican Museum. Photo Alinari

266. FRA BARTOLOMMEO *St. Paul*, Rome, Vatican Museum. Photo Alinari

267. FRA BARTOLOMMEO [with Raphael] *St. Peter* (detail). Photo Anderson

268. FRA BARTOLOMMEO *Study for St. Paul*, Florence, Uffizi. Photo Sopr. alle Gallerie, Florence

269. BUGIARDINI *La Monaca*, Florence, Pitti. Photo Alinari

270. BUGIARDINI *Portrait of a Young Woman*, Paris, Musée Jacquemart-André. Photo Bulloz, Paris

271. BUGIARDINI *Madonna Standing in a Landscape* (sold London, 1946). Photo A. C. Cooper

272. BUGIARDINI *Madonna and Child with St. John* (formerly?) New York, C. H. Holmes Collection. Photo Gray

273. BUGIARDINI *Madonna and Child with St. John* (formerly) London, Agnew. Photo courtesy of the Frick Art Reference Library, New York

274. BUGIARDINI *Madonna del Latte*, Florence, Uffizi. Photo Alinari

275. BUGIARDINI *Ariadne* (?), Venice, Ca' d'Oro. Photo Alinari

276. BUGIARDINI *Leda*, Milan, Treccani Collection. Photo Alinari

277. RIDOLFO GHIRLANDAIO *Portrait of a Lady*, Florence, Pitti. Photo Sopr. alle Gallerie, Florence

278. RIDOLFO GHIRLANDAIO *Adoration of the Child* (destroyed; formerly Berlin, Museums). Photo museum

279. RIDOLFO GHIRLANDAIO *Adoration of the Shepherds*, Budapest, Museum. Photo museum

280. RIDOLFO GHIRLANDAIO *Nativity with Six Saints*, New York, Metropolitan Museum. Photo Anderson

281. RIDOLFO GHIRLANDAIO [shop assistant] *Adoration of the Shepherds* (formerly) London, Henry Harris Collection. Photo A. C. Cooper

282. RIDOLFO GHIRLANDAIO *Madonna della Cintola*, Prato, Cathedral. Photo Alinari

283. RIDOLFO GHIRLANDAIO *Portrait of a Goldsmith*, Florence, Pitti. Photo Sopr. alle Gallerie, Florence

284. RIDOLFO GHIRLANDAIO [with Andrea di Cosimo] *Decoration of Cappella dei Priori*, Florence, Palazzo Vecchio. Photo Alinari

285. RIDOLFO GHIRLANDAIO [with Andrea di Cosimo] *Decoration of Cappella dei Priori*. Photo Alinari

286. GRANACCI *Madonna with Two Saints*, Villamagna (near Florence), S. Donnino. Photo courtesy of Frick Art Reference Library, New York

335. MANCHESTER MASTER *Madonna*, Baden bei Zürich, Private Collection. Photo courtesy of Prof. Federico Zeri, Rome

336. MANCHESTER MASTER *Madonna with St. John and Four Angels*, London, National Gallery. Photo museum. Reproduced by courtesy of the Trustees, The National Gallery, London

337. MANCHESTER MASTER *Madonna*, Florence, Art Market. Photo courtesy of Prof. Federico Zeri, Rome

338. MICHELANGELO [with the Manchester Master] *Entombment*, London National Gallery. Photo museum. Reproduced by courtesy of the Trustees, The National Gallery, London

V

CLIMAX, CRISIS, AND DISSOLUTION OF THE CLASSICAL STYLE IN ROME (*c.* 1514–*c.* 1520)

339. RAPHAEL *Acts of the Apostles* (tapestries), Rome, Vatican Museum (in order of arrangement in the Sistine Chapel). Photos Alinari

340. RAPHAEL *The Stoning of Stephen* (tapestry). Photo Alinari

341. RAPHAEL *The Conversion of Paul* (tapestry). Photo Alinari

342. RAPHAEL *Miraculous Draught of Fishes* (tapestry). Photo Alinari

343. RAPHAEL *Pasce Oves* (tapestry). Photo Alinari

344. RAPHAEL *Blinding of Elymas* (tapestry, fragment). Photo Alinari

345. RAPHAEL *Paul at Lystra* (tapestry). Photo Alinari

346. RAPHAEL *Healing at the Golden Gate* (tapestry). Photo Alinari

347. RAPHAEL *Death of Ananias* (tapestry). Photo Anderson

348. RAPHAEL *Paul Preaching at Athens* (tapestry). Photo Alinari

349. RAPHAEL *Study for the Pasce Oves*, Windsor, Royal Library. Photo Royal Library. Copyright reserved

350. RAPHAEL *Study for the Christ of Pasce Oves*, Paris, Louvre. Photo museum

351. RAPHAEL *Study for the Paul at Lystra*, Chatsworth. Photo Devonshire Collection, Chatsworth. Reproduced by permission the Trustees of the Chatsworth Settlement

352. RAPHAEL *Study for the Blinding of Elymas*, Windsor, Royal Library. Photo Royal Library. Copyright reserved

353. PENNI *Study for the Pasce Oves*, Paris, Louvre. Photo museum

354. PENNI *Study for Paul Preaching at Athens*, Florence, Uffizi. Photo Sopr. alle Gallerie, Florence

355. RAPHAEL *Miraculous Draught of Fishes* (tapestry cartoon), London, Victoria and Albert Museum. Photo museum

356. RAPHAEL *Miraculous Draught of Fishes* (tapestry cartoon, detail). Photo museum

357. RAPHAEL *Miraculous Draught of Fishes* (tapestry cartoon, detail). Photo museum

358. RAPHAEL *Pasce Oves* (tapestry cartoon), London, Victoria and Albert Museum. Photo museum

359. RAPHAEL *Healing at the Golden Gate* (tapestry cartoon), London, Victoria and Albert Museum. Photo museum

360. RAPHAEL *Healing at the Golden Gate* (tapestry cartoon, detail). Photo museum

361. RAPHAEL *Healing at the Golden Gate* (tapestry cartoon, detail). Photo museum

362. RAPHAEL *Death of Ananias* (tapestry cartoon), London, Victoria and Albert Museum. Photo museum

363. RAPHAEL *Death of Ananias* (tapestry cartoon, detail). Photo museum

364. RAPHAEL *Death of Ananias* (tapestry cartoon, detail). Photo museum

365. RAPHAEL *Death of Ananias* (tapestry cartoon, detail). Photo museum

366. RAPHAEL [with Penni] *Blinding of Elymas* (tapestry cartoon), London, Victoria and Albert Museum. Photo museum

367. RAPHAEL *Paul at Lystra* (tapestry cartoon), London, Victoria and Albert Museum. Photo museum

368. RAPHAEL *Paul at Lystra* (tapestry cartoon, detail). Photo museum

369. RAPHAEL [with Penni] *Paul Preaching at Athens* (tapestry cartoon), London, Victoria and Albert Museum. Photo museum

370. PENNI *Paul Preaching at Athens* (tapestry cartoon, detail). Photo museum

371. RAPHAEL *Paul at Lystra* (tapestry cartoon, detail). Photo museum

372. PENNI *Study for the Miraculous Draught of Fishes*, Vienna, Albertina. Photo museum

373. GIULIO [retouched by Raphael?] *Study for the Battle of Ostia*, Vienna, Albertina. Photo museum

374. RAPHAEL [with Giulio] *Battle of Ostia*, Rome, Vatican, Stanza dell'Incendio. Photo Alinari

375. GIULIO *Battle of Ostia* (detail). Photo courtesy of Frick Art Reference Library, New York

376. RAPHAEL [with Giulio] *Fire in the Borgo*, Rome, Vatican, Stanza dell'Incendio. Photo Anderson

377. GIULIO *Fire in the Borgo* (detail). Photo Gabinetto Fotografico Nazionale, Rome

378. GIULIO *Fire in the Borgo* (detail). Photo Archivio Fotografico delle Gallerie e Musei Vaticani

379. GIULIO *Fire in the Borgo* (detail). Photo Archivio Fotografico delle Gallerie e Musei Vaticani

380. RAPHAEL [with Penni] *Coronation of Charlemagne*, Rome, Vatican, Stanza dell'Incendio. Photo Anderson

381. PENNI *Coronation of Charlemagne* (detail). Photo Gabinetto Fotografico Nazionale, Rome

382. PENNI *Study for the Coronation of Charlemagne*, Düsseldorf, Museum. Photo Landesbildstelle Rheinland

383. RAPHAEL [with Penni] *Oath of Leo*, Rome, Vatican, Stanza dell'Incendio. Photo Anderson

384. PENNI *Study for the Oath of Leo*, Florence, Horne Foundation. Photo Sopr. alle Gallerie, Florence

385. GIULIO *Basamento* (detail), Rome, Vatican, Stanza dell'Incendio. Photo Alinari

386. RAPHAEL [with Alvise de Pace] *Cupola of the Cappella Chigi*, Rome, S.M. del Popolo. Photo Alinari

387. RAPHAEL *Study for the Cappella Chigi*, Oxford, Ashmolean. Photo museum. Courtesy of the Visitors of the Ashmolean Museum

388. RAPHAEL *Study for the Cappella Chigi*, Oxford, Ashmolean. Photo museum. Courtesy of the Visitors of the Ashmolean Museum

389. RAPHAEL [with Giovanni da Udine] *Loggetta of the Cardinal Bibbiena*, Rome, Vatican. Photo Archivio Fotografico delle Gallerie e Musei Vaticani

390. RAPHAEL [with Giovanni da Udine] *Loggetta of the Cardinal Bibbiena*. Photo Archivio Fotografico delle Gallerie e Musei Vaticani

391. GIOVANNI DA UDINE [and assistants] *Loggetta of the Cardinal Bibbiena* (detail). Photo Archivio Fotografico delle Gallerie e Musei Vaticani

392. RAPHAEL [with Giovanni da Udine] *Stufetta of the Cardinal Bibbiena*, Rome, Vatican. Photo Archivio Fotografico delle Gallerie e Musei Vaticani

393. RAPHAEL [with Giovanni da Udine] *Stufetta of the Cardinal Bibbiena*. Photo Archivio Fotografico delle Gallerie e Musei Vaticani

394. TADDEO ZUCCARO [and others] *Decoration of the Sala dei Palafrenieri* (free reconstruction of Raphael), Rome, Vatican. Photo Alinari

395. PENNI *Study for the Sala dei Palafrenieri*, Paris, Louvre. Photo museum

396. PENNI *Study for the Sala dei Palafrenieri*, Paris, Louvre. Photo museum

397. RAPHAEL [and assistants] *Sala di Psiche*, Rome, Villa Farnesina. Photo Fototeca di Architettura e Topografia dell'Italia Antica, Rome

398. GIULIO *Three Graces*, Sala di Psiche. Photo Gabinetto Fotografico Nazionale, Rome

399. GIULIO *Venus, Ceres, and Juno*, Sala di Psiche. Photo Alinari

400. GIULIO *Jupiter and Cupid*, Sala di Psiche. Photo Alinari

401. GIULIO *Venus and Psyche*, Sala di Psiche. Photo Alinari

402. RAPHAEL *Study for Venus and Psyche*, Paris, Louvre. Photo museum

403. PENNI *Venus before Jupiter*, Rome, Villa Farnesina, Sala di Psiche. Photo Alinari

404. PENNI *Mercury Descending*, Sala di Psiche. Photo Alinari

405. RAFFAELLINO DEL COLLE (?) *Venus and Cupid*, Sala di Psiche. Photo Alinari

406. GIOVANNI DA UDINE *Amoretto with Mythic Beasts*, Sala di Psiche. Photo Alinari

436. RAPHAEL [with Giulio] *Holy Family of Francis I*, Paris, Louvre. Photo Alinari

437. RAPHAEL [with Giulio] *St. Michael*, Paris, Louvre. Photo Alinari

438. RAPHAEL [and assistants] *Transfiguration*, Rome, Vatican Museum. Photo Anderson

439. PENNI *Transfiguration* (detail). Photo Anderson

440. RAPHAEL [and Giulio] *Transfiguration* (detail). Photo Alinari

441. GIULIO *Transfiguration* (detail). Photo Alinari

442. RAPHAEL *Transfiguration* (detail), *St. Andrew*. Photo Alinari

443. RAPHAEL *Study for St. Andrew*, London, British Museum. Photo museum. Courtesy of the Trustees of the British Museum

444. RAPHAEL *Study for the Transfiguration*, Oxford, Ashmolean. Photo museum. Courtesy of the Visitors of the Ashmolean Museum

445. GIULIO (?) *Study for the Transfiguration*, Paris, Louvre. Photo Alinari

446. GIULIO *Madonna Piccola Gonzaga*, Paris, Louvre. Photo Archives Photographiques, Paris

447. GIULIO *St. Margaret*, Paris, Louvre. Photo Alinari

448. GIULIO *Madonna della Perla*, Madrid, Prado. Photo Anderson

449. PENNI *Visitation*, Madrid, Prado. Photo Anderson

450. PENNI *Madonna del Divino Amore*, Naples, Galleria Nazionale. Photo Brogi

451. GIULIO [with Penni] *St. John Baptist*, Florence, Academy. Photo Sopr. alle Gallerie, Florence

452. GIULIO [with Raffaellino] *Madonna della Rosa*, Madrid, Prado. Photo Anderson

453. GIULIO [with Raffaellino] *Madonna of the Oak*, Madrid, Prado. Photo MAS, Barcelona

454. GIULIO [with Raffaellino] *St. Margaret*, Vienna, Kunsthistorisches Museum. Photo Wolfrum

455. SEBASTIANO *Man in Armor*, Hartford, Atheneum. Courtesy of Mr. H. Sperling, New York

456. SEBASTIANO *Young Violinist*, Paris, Baron G. de Rothschild. Photo Archives Photographiques, Paris

457. SEBASTIANO *Portrait of a Young Man*, Budapest, Museum. Photo museum

458. SEBASTIANO *Cardinal Antonio Ciocchi del Monte Sansovino*, Dublin, National Gallery. Photo museum. Courtesy of the National Gallery of Ireland

459. SEBASTIANO *Verdelotti and Ubretto* (destroyed; formerly Berlin, Museums). Photo museum

460. SEBASTIANO *Cardinal Bandinello Sauli and Suite*, Washington, National Gallery, Kress Collection. Photo Samuel H. Kress Collection

461. SEBASTIANO *Pietà*, Viterbo, Museum. Photo Gabinetto Fotografico Nazionale, Rome

462. SEBASTIANO *Pietà*, Leningrad, Hermitage. Photo museum

540. FRA BARTOLOMMEO *Isaiah*, Florence, Academy. Photo Anderson

541. FRA BARTOLOMMEO *Job*, Florence, Academy. Photo Anderson

542. FRA BARTOLOMMEO [with Fra Paolino] *Assumption of the Virgin*, Naples, Galleria Nazionale. Photo Alinari

543. FRA BARTOLOMMEO *Study for the Assumption*, Munich, Graphische Sammlung. Photo museum

544. FRA BARTOLOMMEO *Holy Family*, Rome, Galleria Nazionale. Photo Alinari

545. FRA BARTOLOMMEO *Madonna and Child with Elizabeth and John*, London, Kenwood, Iveagh Bequest. Photo courtesy of the Trustees of the Cook Collection

546. FRA BARTOLOMMEO [with Bugiardini] *Pietà*, Florence, Pitti. Photo Alinari

547. FRA BARTOLOMMEO *Noli Me Tangere*, Le Caldine, Convento della Maddalena. Photo Alinari

548. FRA PAOLINO *Crucifixion*, Siena, Sto. Spirito. Photo Alinari

549. FRA PAOLINO *Holy Family with St. John and Angels*, Rome, Galleria Doria. Photo Gabinetto Fotografico Nazionale, Rome

550. FRA PAOLINO *Pietà*, Florence, Museo di S. Marco. Photo Alinari

551. ANDREA DEL SARTO *Scenes from the Life of St. John Baptist*, Florence, Scalzo. Photo author

552. ANDREA DEL SARTO *Preaching of St. John Baptist*, Florence, Scalzo. Photo Brogi

553. ANDREA DEL SARTO *Justice*, Florence, Scalzo. Photo Alinari

554. ANDREA DEL SARTO *Charity*, Florence, Scalzo. Photo Brogi

555. ANDREA DEL SARTO *Chiaroscuro Panel* (from the Leo X Festival Decoration?), Florence, Uffizi. Photo Sopr. alle Gallerie, Florence

556. ANDREA DEL SARTO *Chiaroscuro Panel* (from the Leo X Festival Decoration?), Florence, Uffizi. Photo Sopr. alle Gallerie, Florence

557. ANDREA DEL SARTO *Chiaroscuro Panel* (from the Leo X Festival Decoration?), Florence, Uffizi. Photo Sopr. alle Gallerie, Florence

558. ANDREA DEL SARTO *Holy Family with St. Catherine*, Leningrad, Hermitage. Photo museum

559. A. VENEZIANO [after Andrea del Sarto] *Pietà*. Photo courtesy of Metropolitan Museum of Art, Whittelsey Fund

560. ANDREA DEL SARTO *Study for the Pietà*, Florence, Uffizi. Photo Alinari

561. ANDREA DEL SARTO *Redeemer*, Florence, SS. Annunziata. Photo Alinari

562. ANDREA DEL SARTO *Holy Family*, Paris, Louvre 1515. Photo Alinari

563. ANDREA DEL SARTO *Baptism of the Multitude*, Florence, Scalzo. Photo Brogi

564. ANDREA DEL SARTO *Capture of St. John*, Florence, Scalzo. Photo Brogi

565. ANDREA DEL SARTO *Madonna of the Harpies*, Florence, Uffizi. Photo Brogi

566. ANDREA DEL SARTO *Disputation on the Trinity*, Florence, Pitti. Photo Anderson

567. ANDREA DEL SARTO *Portrait of a Sculptor*(?), London, National Gallery. Photo museum. Reproduced by courtesy of the Trustees, The National Gallery, London

568. ANDREA DEL SARTO *Study for Portrait of a Sculptor*, Florence, Uffizi. Photo Sopr. alle Gallerie, Florence

569. ANDREA DEL SARTO *Caritas*, Paris, Louvre. Photo Alinari

570. ANDREA DEL SARTO *Madonna and Child with St. John*, Rome, Borghese 334. Photo Anderson

571. ANDREA DEL SARTO *Madonna with St. John and Angels* (?), London, Wallace Collection. Photo reproduced by permission of the Trustees of the Wallace Collection

572. ANDREA DEL SARTO *Pietà*, Vienna, Kunsthistorisches Museum. Photo Wolfrum

573. ANDREA DEL SARTO *Tribute to Caesar* (in its original dimensions), Poggio a Cajano. Photo Alinari

574. FRANCIABIGIO *Annunciation*, Turin, Galleria Sabauda. Photo Alinari

575. FRANCIABIGIO *Angel*, Florence, Sto. Spirito. Photo Brogi

576. FRANCIABIGIO *St. Job Altar*, Florence, Uffizi. Photo Brogi

577. FRANCIABIGIO *Meeting of Christ and St. John Baptist*, Florence, Scalzo. Photo Alinari

578. FRANCIABIGIO *Madonna and Child with St. John*, Vienna, Kunsthistorisches Museum 208. Photo museum

579. FRANCIABIGIO *Benediction of St. John by Zachary*, Florence, Scalzo. Photo Alinari

580. FRANCIABIGIO *Leda*, Brussels, Museum. Photo copyright A.C.L. Brussels

581. FRANCIABIGIO *Madonna*, Bologna, Pinacoteca 294. Photo Anderson

582. FRANCIABIGIO *Triumph of Caesar* (in its original dimensions), Poggio a Cajano. Photo Alinari

583. FRANCIABIGIO *Self-Portrait*, New York, Hunter College, ex Kress Collection. Photo Samuel H. Kress Collection, New York

584. FRANCIABIGIO *Portrait of Caradosso*, London, Art Market. Photo A. C. Cooper

585. FRANCIABIGIO *Portrait of a Man*, Vienna, Liechtenstein Collection. Photo Wolfrum

586. FRANCIABIGIO *Portrait of a Fattore*, Hampton Court. Photo Hampton Court. Copyright reserved

587. BUGIARDINI *Temptation in the Garden of Eden*, New York, Private Collection. Photo courtesy of Duveen Brothers, New York

588. BUGIARDINI *St. Sebastian*, New York, Kress Collection. Photo Samuel H. Kress Collection, New York

589. BUGIARDINI *Madonna and Child with the Infant St. John*, Dunblane, Stirling Collection. Photo Talani, Florence

590. BUGIARDINI *Madonna and Child with the Infant St. John*, Florence, Uffizi. Photo Anderson

591. BUGIARDINI *Madonna and Child with the Infant St. John*, Allentown (Pennsylvania), Museum, Kress Collection. Photo Samuel H. Kress Collection, New York

592. RIDOLFO GHIRLANDAIO *Coronation of the Virgin*, Florence, S.M. Novella, Cappella del Papa. Photo Brogi

593. RIDOLFO GHIRLANDAIO *Resuscitation of a Youth by St. Zenobius*, Florence, Academy. Photo Anderson

594. RIDOLFO GHIRLANDAIO *Translation of the Body of St. Zenobius*, Florence, Academy. Photo Anderson

595. RIDOLFO GHIRLANDAIO *Madonna with Six Saints*, Pistoia, Museum. Photo Brogi

596. RIDOLFO GHIRLANDAIO *Girolamo Benivieni* (?), London, National Gallery. Photo Anderson

597. RIDOLFO GHIRLANDAIO *Portrait of a Man*, Florence, Galleria Corsini. Photo Alinari

598. RIDOLFO GHIRLANDAIO *Portrait of a Man*, Florence, Torrigiani Collection. Photo Talani, Florence

599. RIDOLFO GHIRLANDAIO *Pietà*, Colle di Val d'Elsa, S. Agostino. Photo Brogi

600. GRANACCI *Madonna with Sts. Francis and Zenobius*, Florence, Academy. Photo Alinari

601. GRANACCI *Holy Family*, Boughton House, Duke of Buccleuch. Photo Ideal Studios, Edinburgh. Courtesy of the Duke of Buccleuch

602. GRANACCI *Madonna and Child*, San Francisco, Palace of the Legion of Honor. Photo museum

603. GRANACCI *Sts. John, Apollonia, Mary Magdalen, and Jerome* (from the *Apollonia Altar*), Munich, Pinakothek. Photo museum

604. GRANACCI *Predella Panel* (from the *Apollonia Altar*), Florence, Academy. Photo Sopr. alle Gallerie, Florence

605. GRANACCI *Predella Panel* (from the *Apollonia Altar*), Florence, Academy. Photo Sopr. alle Gallerie, Florence

606. GRANACCI *Predella Panel* (from the *Apollonia Altar*), Florence, Academy. Photo Sopr. alle Gallerie, Florence

607. GRANACCI *Entry of Charles VIII into Florence*, Florence, Museo Mediceo. Photo Anderson

608. GRANACCI *Joseph Presents His Father to Pharaoh*, Florence, Uffizi. Photo Alinari

609. GRANACCI *Arrest of Joseph*, Florence, Uffizi. Photo Alinari

610. GRANACCI *Madonna with St. John*, (formerly) Munich, A. S. Drey. Photo courtesy of Drey Galleries, New York

611. GRANACCI *Madonna with Four Saints*, Montemurlo, Pieve. Photo Sopr. alle Gallerie, Florence

612. SOGLIANI *Madonna with St. John*, Baltimore, Walters Art Gallery. Photo courtesy of Walters Art Gallery

613. SOGLIANI *Madonna with St. John*, Brussels, Museum. Photo copyright A.C.L. Brussels

614. SOGLIANI *Madonna with St. John*, Turin, Galleria Sabauda. Photo Alinari

615. SOGLIANI *S. Acasio Altar*, Florence, S. Lorenzo. Photo Alinari

616. SOGLIANI *S. Brigitta Altar*, Florence, Academy. Photo Alinari

617. PULIGO [on Sarto's cartoon] *Holy Family*, London, National Gallery. Photo museum. Reproduced by courtesy of the Trustees, The National Gallery, London

618. ANDREA [with Puligo] *Story of Joseph* (1), Florence, Pitti 87. Photo Brogi

619. ANDREA [with Puligo] *Story of Joseph* (2), Florence, Pitti 88. Photo Sopr. alle Gallerie, Florence

620. PULIGO *Madonna with St. John*, Florence, Pitti 242. Photo Alinari

621. PULIGO *Madonna with St. John and Angels*, Florence, Galleria Corsini. Photo Brogi

622. PULIGO *Adoration of the Kings* (formerly) Milan, Crespi Collection. Photo Anderson

623. PULIGO *Deposition*, Venice, Seminario. Photo Anderson

624. PULIGO *Preaching of St. John Baptist* (formerly) London, Henry Harris Collection. Photo A. C. Cooper

625. PULIGO *History of Joseph*, Rome, Borghese 463. Photo Sopr. alle Gallerie, Florence

626. PULIGO *Apollo and Daphne*, Florence, Galleria Corsini. Photo Alinari

627. BACCHIACCA *Deposition*, Bassano, Museo Civico. Photo Alinari

628. BACCHIACCA *Adam and Eve*, Philadelphia Museum, Johnson Collection. Photo courtesy of John G. Johnson Collection, Philadelphia

629. BACCHIACCA *Story of Joseph*, London, National Gallery 1218. Photo museum. Reproduced by courtesy of the Trustees, The National Gallery, London

630. BACCHIACCA *Story of Joseph*, Rome, Borghese. Photo Sopr. alle Gallerie, Florence

631. BACCHIACCA *Story of Joseph*, London, National Gallery 1219. Photo museum. Reproduced by courtesy of the Trustees, The National Gallery, London

632. BACCHIACCA *Story of Joseph*, Rome, Borghese. Photo Sopr. alle Gallerie, Florence

633. BACCHIACCA *Deposition*, Florence, Uffizi. Photo Brogi

634. BACCHIACCA *Creation of Eve*, Stockholm, Private Collection. Photo Talani, Florence

635. BACCHIACCA   *Leda*, Rotterdam, Boymans Museum, van Beuningen Collection. Photo museum

636. BACCHIACCA   *Predella Panel* (from the *S. Acasio Altar*), Florence, Uffizi. Photo Anderson

637. BACCHIACCA   *Predella Panel* (from the *S. Acasio Altar*), Florence, Uffizi. Photo Anderson

638. BACCHIACCA   *Legend of the Dead King*, Dresden, Gallery. Photo Alinari

639. PONTORMO   *Visitation*, Florence, SS. Annunziata. Photo Sopr. alle Gallerie, Florence

640. PONTORMO   *Visitation* (detail). Photo Sopr. alle Gallerie, Florence

641. PONTORMO   *Cappella del Papa* (vault), Florence, S.M. Novella. Photo Brogi

642. PONTORMO   *St. Veronica*, Florence, S.M. Novella, Cappella del Papa. Photo Sopr. alle Gallerie, Florence

643. PONTORMO   *Joseph Revealing Himself to His Brothers*, Henfield, Lady Salmond. Photo Sopr. alle Gallerie, Florence

644. PONTORMO   *Joseph Sold to Potiphar*, Henfield, Lady Salmond. Photo Sopr. alle Gallerie, Florence

645. PONTORMO   *The Butler Restored and the Baker Led to Execution*, Henfield, Lady Salmond. Photo Sopr. alle Gallerie, Florence

646. PONTORMO   *Madonna and Saints*, Florence, S. Michele Visdomini. Photo Sopr. alle Gallerie, Florence

647. PONTORMO   *Pietà* (predella for the Visdomini Altar), Dublin, National Gallery. Photo museum. Courtesy of the National Gallery of Ireland

648. PONTORMO   *St. Lawrence* (portion of predella), Dublin, National Gallery. Photo museum. Courtesy of the National Gallery of Ireland

649. PONTORMO   *St. Francis* (portion of predella), Dublin, National Gallery. Photo museum. Courtesy of the National Gallery of Ireland

650. PONTORMO   *Joseph in Egypt*, London, National Gallery. Photo museum. Reproduced by courtesy of the Trustees, The National Gallery, London

651. PONTORMO   *Cosimo de' Medici*, Florence, Uffizi. Photo Sopr. alle Gallerie, Florence

652. PONTORMO   *Study for a Portrait of Piero de' Medici*, Rome, Galleria Corsini. Photo Sopr. alle Gallerie, Florence

653. PONTORMO   *Portrait of a Musician* [Francesco dell'Ajolle?], Florence, Uffizi. Photo Sopr. alle Gallerie, Florence

654. PONTORMO   *Study for St. John Evangelist*, Florence, Uffizi. Photo Sopr. alle Gallerie, Florence

655. PONTORMO   *St. John Evangelist*, Empoli, Collegiata. Photo Sopr. alle Gallerie, Florence

656. PONTORMO   *St. Michael*, Empoli, Collegiata. Photo Sopr. alle Gallerie, Florence

657. PONTORMO   *Study for a Pietà*, Florence, Uffizi. Photo Sopr. alle Gallerie, Florence

VII

EPILOGUE: THE ASCENDANCY OF MANNERISM
(*some events of 1521*)

I

INTRODUCTION

THE GENESIS
OF HIGH RENAISSANCE
CLASSICAL STYLE

1. LEONARDO *Head of an Angel*, from Verrocchio's *Baptism of Christ*, Florence, Uffizi

2. VERROCCHIO *Baptism of Christ*, Florence, Uffizi

3. LEONARDO *Adoration of the Magi*, Florence, Uffizi

4. LEONARDO *Adoration of the Magi* (detail)

5. LEONARDO *Adoration of the Magi* (detail)

7

6. DOMENICO GHIRLANDAIO
Adoration of the Magi,
Florence, Innocenti

7. ANTONIO POLLAIUOLO   *Hercules and the Hydra*, *Hercules and Anteus* (lost; formerly
Florence, Uffizi)

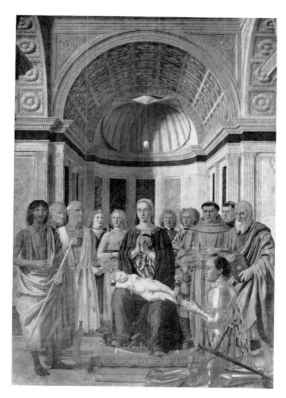

8. PIERO DELLA FRANCESCA
Montefeltro Altar, Milan, Brera

9. BOTTICELLI   *Adoration of the Magi*, Florence, Uffizi

10. LEONARDO *Virgin of the Rocks*, Paris, Louvre

11. LEONARDO *Virgin of the Rocks* (detail)

12. LEONARDO *Last Supper*, Milan, S.M. delle Grazie

13. LEONARDO *Last Supper* (detail)

14. FILIPPINO LIPPI *Adoration of the Magi*, Florence, Uffizi

13

15. PIERO DI COSIMO   *Mars and Venus*, Berlin, Museums

16. PERUGINO   *Vision of St. Bernard*, Munich, Pinakothek

17. MICHELANGELO
Madonna of the Steps, Florence,
Casa Buonarroti

18. MICHELANGELO   *Battle of the Centaurs*, Florence, Casa Buonarroti

19. MICHELANGELO *Pietà*, Rome, St. Peter's

20. MICHELANGELO *Bacchus*, Florence, Bargello

21. FRA BARTOLOMMEO [with Albertinelli]   *Last Judgment*, Florence, Museo di S. Marco

I I

FORMATION OF THE
CLASSICAL VOCABULARY

(c. 1500-c. 1508)

22. LEONARDO *St. Anne Cartoon*, London, Royal Academy

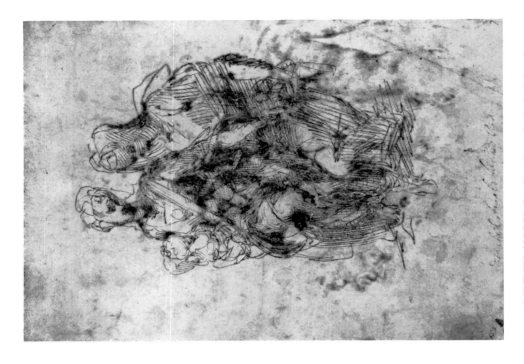

24. MICHELANGELO *St. Anne*, Oxford, Ashmolean

23. ANDREA DEL BRESCIANINO *St. Anne* (destroyed; formerly Berlin, Museums)

22

26. MICHELANGELO *David*, Florence, Academy

25. MICHELANGELO *Bruges Madonna*, Bruges, Notre Dame

23

27. MICHELANGELO *Doni Holy Family*, Florence, Uffizi

28. LEONARDO *Battle of the Standard* (copy), Florence, Palazzo Vecchio

29. RUBENS *Battle of the Standard* (copy after Leonardo), Paris, Louvre

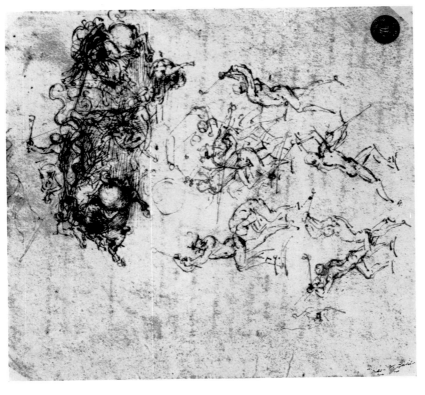

30, 31. LEONARDO *Studies for the Battle of Anghiari*, Venice, Academy

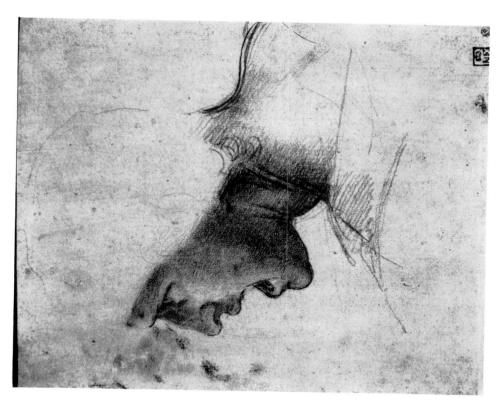

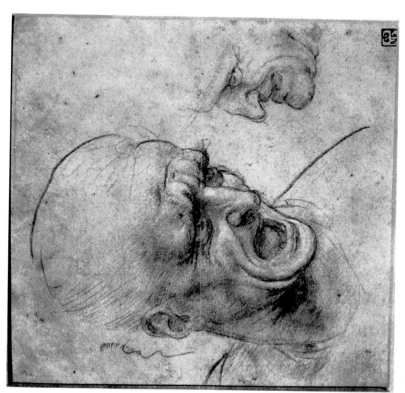

32, 33. LEONARDO *Studies for the Battle of Anghiari*, Budapest, Museum

34. MICHELANGELO
St. Matthew, Florence, Academy

35. MICHELANGELO *Study for the Julius Tomb* (incorporating the lower story of the project of 1505[?]; copy), Florence, Uffizi

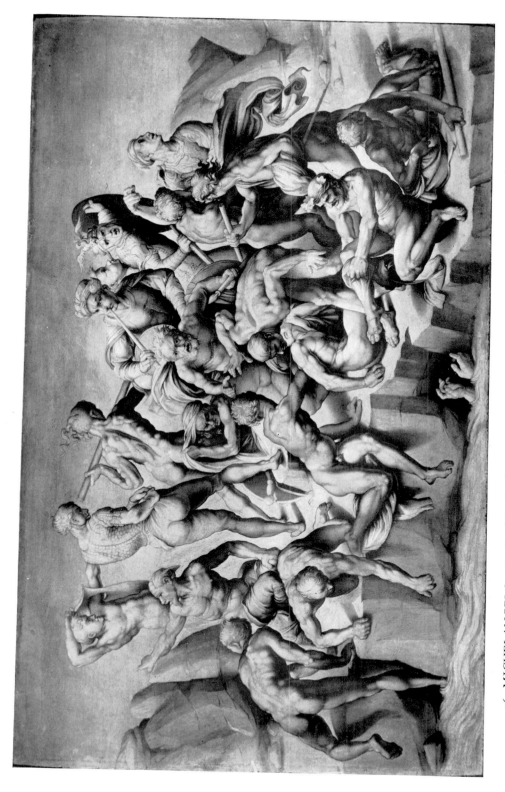

36. MICHELANGELO *Battle of Cascina* (central portion); copy attributed to Aristotile da Sangallo, Holkham Hall

29

37. LEONARDO *Mona Lisa*, Paris, Louvre

38. LEONARDO *Mona Lisa* (detail)

39. LEONARDO *St. Anne, Virgin, and Child*, Paris, Louvre

40. ALBERTINELLI *Madonna and Saints* (portable triptych), Milan, Poldi–Pezzoli

41. ALBERTINELLI *Crucifixion*, Florence, Certosa

33

42. ALBERTINELLI *Visitation*, Florence, Uffizi

34

43. FRA BARTOLOMMEO   *Vision of St. Bernard*, Florence, Academy

45. FRA BARTOLOMMEO *Noli Me Tangere*, Paris, Louvre

44. FILIPPINO LIPPI *Vision of St. Bernard*, Florence, Badia

46. FRA BARTOLOMMEO [with Albertinelli] *Assumption of the Virgin* (destroyed; formerly Berlin, Museums)

47. ALBERTINELLI *Annunciation with Sts. Sebastian and Lucy*, Munich, Pinakothek

48. RAPHAEL *Three Graces*, Chantilly, Musée Condé

49. RAPHAEL *Marriage of the Virgin*, Milan, Brera

50. RAPHAEL *Madonna del Granduca*, Florence, Pitti

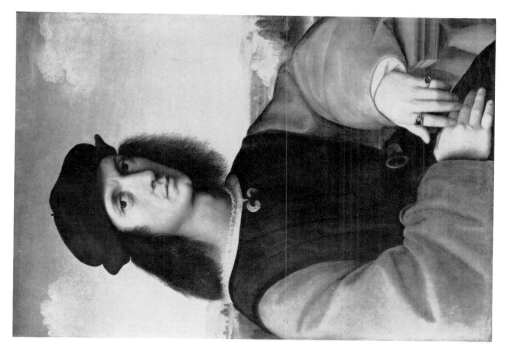

52. RAPHAEL *Angelo Doni*, Florence, Pitti

51. RAPHAEL *Maddalena Doni*, Florence, Pitti

41

53. RAPHAEL *Madonna del Prato*, Vienna, Kunsthistorisches Museum

54. RAPHAEL *Madonna del Cardellino*, Florence, Uffizi

42

55. RAPHAEL   *La Belle Jardinière*, Paris, Louvre

57. RAPHAEL *Madonna Study*, Paris, Louvre

56. RAPHAEL *Bridgewater House Madonna*, Edinburgh,
National Gallery, Ellesmere Loan

59. RAPHAEL *Entombment*, Rome, Borghese

58. RAPHAEL *Holy Family of the Casa Canigiani*, Munich, Pinakothek

45

60. RAPHAEL *Madonna del Baldacchino*, Florence, Pitti

61. RAFFAELLINO CARLI *Madonna with Saints*, Florence, Sto. Spirito

62. LORENZO DI CREDI *Madonna with Saints*, Pistoia, S.M. delle Grazie

64. PIERO DI COSIMO *Immaculate Conception*, Florence, Uffizi

63. PIERO DI COSIMO *Madonna with Saints*, Florence, Innocenti

48

65. PIERO DI COSIMO *Madonna with St. John*, Vienna, Liechtenstein Collection

66. PIERO DI COSIMO *Liberation of Andromeda*, Florence, Uffizi 1536

67. GRANACCI *Holy Family*, Washington, National Gallery, Kress Collection

68. GRANACCI *Madonna with Two Saints*, Berlin, Museums

69. GRANACCI *Holy Family with St. John*, Dublin, National Gallery

71. BUGIARDINI *Madonna and Child with St. John*, New York, Metropolitan Museum

70. GRANACCI *Madonna della Cintola*, Florence, Academy

73. BUGIARDINI *Portrait of a Lady*, Urbino, Galleria Nazionale

72. BUGIARDINI *Holy Family*, Turin, Galleria Sabauda

75. RIDOLFO GHIRLANDAIO *Coronation of the Virgin,*
Paris, Louvre

74. RIDOLFO GHIRLANDAIO *Madonna with Sts. Francis and Mary Magdalen,*
Florence, Academy

55

78, 79. RIDOLFO GHIRLANDAIO *Altar Wings with Angels*, Florence, Academy

81. RIDOLFO GHIRLANDAIO *Lady with a Rabbit*, New Haven, Yale University Art Gallery

80. RIDOLFO GHIRLANDAIO *Portrait of a Man*, Chicago, Art Institute

82. RIDOLFO GHIRLANDAIO *Girl with a Unicorn*, Rome, Borghese

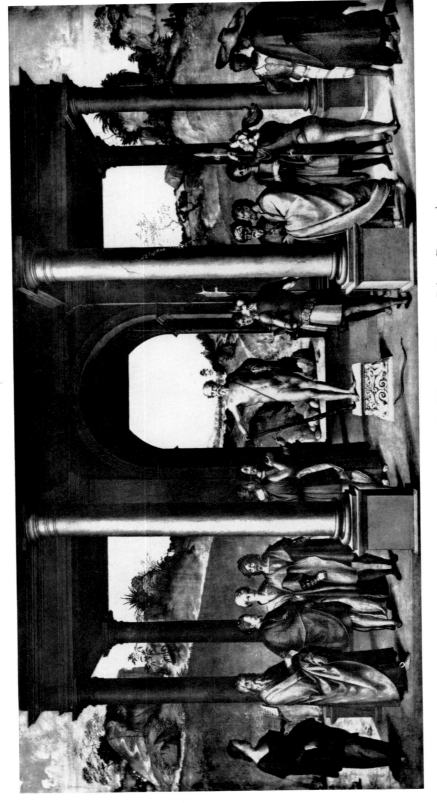

83. FRANCIABIGIO *Temple of Hercules*, Florence, Palazzo Davanzati

85. FRANCIABIGIO *Madonna*, Perugia, Count Ranieri

84. FRANCIABIGIO *Madonna and Child with St. John*, Florence, Uffizi 2178

87. FRANCIABIGIO *Madonna del Pozzo*, Florence, Academy

86. FRANCIABIGIO *Holy Family*, Florence, Academy (ex–Uffizi 888)

88. FRANCIABIGIO *Holy Family*, Vienna, Kunsthistorisches Museum 206

89. PINTURICCHIO *Choir Vault*, Rome, S.M. del Popolo

90. [Anon.] *Sibyls*, Rome, S. Pietro in Montorio

91. PERUZZI [and others] *Choir Decoration*, Rome, S. Onofrio

92. PERUZZI (?) *Coronation of the Virgin*, Rome, S. Onofrio

93. PERUZZI *Decoration of the Chapel*, Castello di Belcaro

94. PERUZZI *Madonna with Saints* (altar fresco), Rome, S. Onofrio

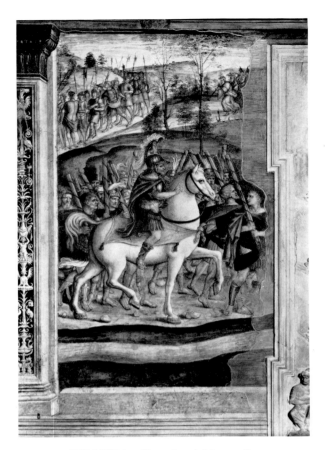

95. RIPANDA   *Consul and Lictors*, Rome,
Palazzo dei Conservatori

96. SODOMA   *Central Octagon of the Stanza della Segnatura*, Rome, Vatican

III

THE MATURITY OF THE CLASSICAL STYLE IN ROME
(c. 1508-c. 1514)

97. MICHELANGELO *The Sistine Ceiling*, Rome, Vatican, Sistine Chapel

98. MICHELANGELO *The Sistine Ceiling* (central bays)

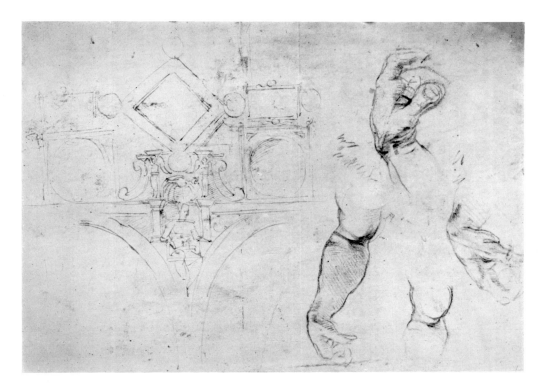

99. MICHELANGELO *Preliminary Plan for Sistine Ceiling*, London, British Museum

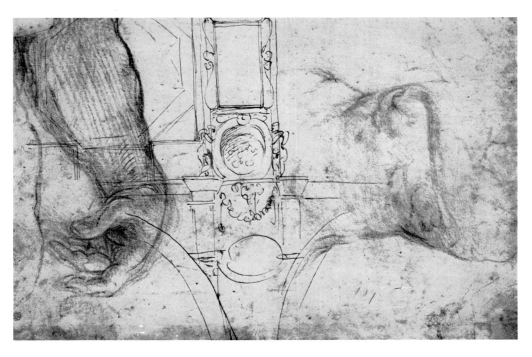

100. MICHELANGELO *Preliminary Plan for Sistine Ceiling*, Detroit, Institute of Arts

101, 102. MICHELANGELO *Bronze-colored Nudes in the Spandrels*, Sistine Ceiling

103. MICHELANGELO *The Flood*, Sistine Ceiling

105. MICHELANGELO *Drunkenness of Noah*, Sistine Ceiling

107. MICHELANGELO *Prophet Joel*, Sistine Ceiling

106. MICHELANGELO *Delphic Sibyl*, Sistine Ceiling

109. MICHELANGELO *Erithrean Sibyl*, Sistine Ceiling

108. MICHELANGELO *Prophet Zachary*, Sistine Ceiling

79

ESAIAS

110. MICHELANGELO *Prophet Isaiah*, Sistine Ceiling

III. MICHELANGELO *Ignudi around the Drunkenness of Noah*, Sistine Ceiling

112, 113. MICHELANGELO *Ignudi above Prophet Joel*, Sistine Ceiling

114. MICHELANGELO *Ignudi around Sacrifice of Noah,* Sistine Ceiling

115, 116. MICHELANGELO *Ignudi above Prophet Isaiah*, Sistine Ceiling

117. MICHELANGELO *Creation of Eve*, Sistine Ceiling

118. MICHELANGELO *Ignudi around Creation of Eve*, Sistine Ceiling

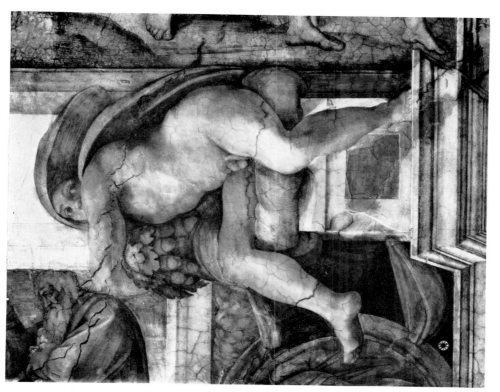

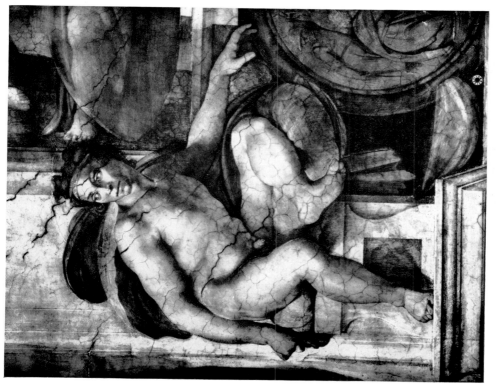

119, 120. MICHELANGELO *Ignudi above Cumaean Sibyl*, Sistine Ceiling

121. MICHELANGELO *Temptation and Expulsion*, Sistine Ceiling

122. MICHELANGELO *Creation of Adam*, Sistine Ceiling

123. MICHELANGELO *Creation of Adam* (detail), Sistine Ceiling

124. MICHELANGELO *Creation of the Sun and Moon, Sistine Ceiling*

125. MICHELANGELO *Separation of Earth and Waters*, Sistine Ceiling

126. MICHELANGELO *Separation of Light and Darkness*, Sistine Ceiling

127. MICHELANGELO *Ignudi around Separation of Earth and Waters*, Sistine Ceiling

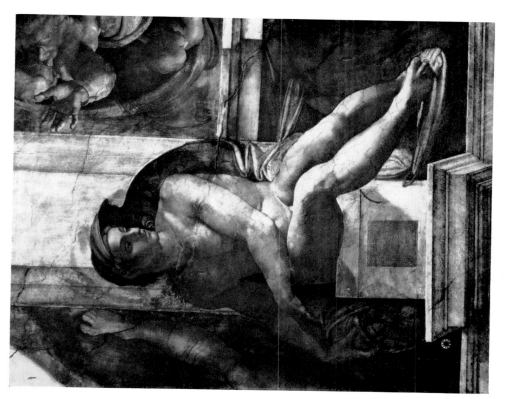

128, 129. MICHELANGELO *Ignudi above Persian Sibyl*, Sistine Ceiling

130. MICHELANGELO *Ignudi around Separation of Light and Darkness*, Sistine Ceiling

131, 132. MICHELANGELO *Ignudi above Prophet Jeremiah*, Sistine Ceiling

97

134. MICHELANGELO *Persian Sibyl*, Sistine Ceiling

133. MICHELANGELO *Cumaean Sibyl*, Sistine Ceiling

98

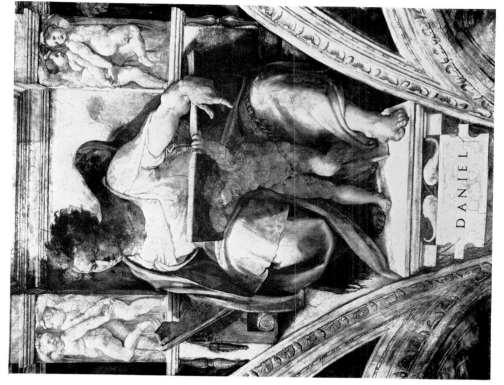

136. MICHELANGELO *Prophet Daniel*, Sistine Ceiling

135. MICHELANGELO *Prophet Ezekiel*, Sistine Ceiling

137. MICHELANGELO *Libyan Sibyl*, Sistine Ceiling

138. MICHELANGELO *Prophet Jonah*, Sistine Ceiling

HIEREMIAS

139. MICHELANGELO *Prophet Jeremiah*, Sistine Ceiling

140. MICHELANGELO *David and Goliath*, Sistine Ceiling

141. MICHELANGELO *Judith and Holofernes*, Sistine Ceiling

142. MICHELANGELO *The Hanging of Haman*, Sistine Ceiling

143. MICHELANGELO *The Brazen Serpent, Sistine Ceiling*

144. MICHELANGELO *Ancestors of Christ*, Sistine Ceiling, severies

146. MICHELANGELO *Ancestors of Christ*, Sistine Ceiling, lunettes

145. MICHELANGELO *Ancestors of Christ*, Sistine Ceiling, severies

147. MICHELANGELO *Ancestors of Christ*, Sistine Ceiling, lunettes

148. MICHELANGELO *Ancestors of Christ*, Sistine Ceiling

149. RAPHAEL *Stanza della Segnatura*, Rome, Vatican

150. RAPHAEL *Stanza della Segnatura*

151. RAPHAEL [and Sodoma]   *Ceiling of the Stanza della Segnatura*

152. RAPHAEL   *Poetry*, Stanza della Segnatura, ceiling

153. RAPHAEL   *Justice*, Stanza della Segnatura, ceiling

155. RAPHAEL *The Judgment of Solomon, Stanza della Segnatura, ceiling*

154. RAPHAEL *The Flaying of Marsyas, Stanza della Segnatura, ceiling*

156. RAPHAEL *Disputà*, Stanza della Segnatura

157. RAPHAEL *Disputà* (detail)

158. RAPHAEL *Disputà* (detail)

159. RAPHAEL *Parnassus*, Stanza della Segnatura

160. RAPHAEL *Parnassus* (detail), *Apollo and Muses*

161. RAPHAEL   *Parnassus* (detail), *Sappho and Other Poets*

162. RAPHAEL   *Parnassus* (detail), *Modern Poets*

163. RAPHAEL, *School of Athens*, Stanza della Segnatura

164. RAPHAEL   *School of Athens* (detail), *Plato and Aristotle*

165. RAPHAEL   *School of Athens* (detail), *Pythagorean Group*

166. RAPHAEL *School of Athens* (detail), *Euclidian Group*

167. RAPHAEL
School of Athens (detail), *Heraclitus*

168. RAPHAEL   *Cartoon for School of Athens* (detail), Milan, Ambrosiana

169. RAPHAEL *Cartoon for School of Athens*, Milan, Ambrosiana

170. RAPHAEL *The Law*, Stanza della Segnatura

171. RAPHAEL   *The Three Virtues of Justice, Stanza della Segnatura*

172. RAPHAEL *Handing over of the Decretals*, Stanza della Segnatura

173. RAPHAEL *The Civil Law*,
Stanza della Segnatura

174. RAPHAEL [with Penni] *Grisaille and Grotesque Decoration* (beneath *Parnassus*), Stanza
della Segnatura

175. RAPHAEL *Madonna di Casa Alba*, Washington, National Gallery

176. RAPHAEL *Study for Alba Madonna*, Lille, Musée Wicar

177. RAPHAEL *Madonna di Foligno*, Rome, Vatican Museum

178. RAPHAEL *Isaiah*, Rome, S. Agostino

132

179. RIPANDA (?) *Triumph of Titus*, Paris, Louvre 180

180. [Anon.] *Façade Decoration of the Casa Sander*, Rome

181. [Anon.] *Façade Decoration*, Via Maschera d'Oro no. 9, Rome

182. PERUZZI *Three Graces*, San Francisco, Zellerbach Collection

183. PERUZZI *Sala di Galatea*, Rome, Villa Farnesina

184. PERUZZI *Aquarius between the Swan and Dolphin*. SEBASTIANO *Tireus and Philomel;*
The Daughters of Cecrops, Sala di Galatea

185. PERUZZI *Perseus-Pegasus*, Sala di Galatea

186. PERUZZI *Ursa Major*, Sala di Galatea

187. PERUZZI *Luna in Virgo, Bacchus and Ariadne, Mars in Libra near Scorpio.*
SEBASTIANO *Fall of Phaeton*, Sala di Galatea

188. PERUZZI *Venus in Capricorn with Sagittarius and Lyra*,
Sala di Galatea

189. PERUZZI   *Argo*, Sala di Galatea

190. PERUZZI   *Sol in Sagittarius*, Sala di Galatea

141

191. PERUZZI *Death of Meleager*, Rome, Villa Farnesina, Sala del Fregio

192. PERUZZI *Hunting of Calydonian Boar*, Sala del Fregio

193. PERUZZI *Nymph and Satyrs ; Slaying of Marsyas* (portions), Sala del Fregio

194. SODOMA *Marriage of Alexander and Roxane*, Rome, Villa Farnesina

195. SODOMA *Alexander and the Family of Darius; The Forge of Vulcan*, Rome, Villa Farnesina

196. SEBASTIANO *Juno*, Sala di Galatea, Rome, Villa Farnesina

197. SEBASTIANO *Fall of Icarus*, Sala di Galatea

198. SEBASTIANO *Polyphemus*, Sala di Galatea

199. SEBASTIANO *Adoration of the Shepherds*, Cambridge, Fitzwilliam Museum

200. SEBASTIANO *Death of Adonis*, Florence, Uffizi

201. SEBASTIANO *Madonna and Child*, London, Pouncey Collection

203. SEBASTIANO *Portrait of a Girl* (called "Dorothea"),
Berlin, Museums

202. SEBASTIANO *Portrait of a Girl* (called "La Fornarina"),
Florence, Uffizi

204. PERUZZI *Giant Head*, Sala di Galatea, Rome, Villa Farnesina

205. PERUZZI *Ceiling of the Stanza d'Eliodoro*, Rome, Vatican

153

206. PERUZZI (?) *Project for Stanza d'Eliodoro*, Paris, Louvre

207. PERUZZI *Study for Ceiling*, Stanza d'Eliodoro; Oxford, Ashmolean

208. PERUZZI *Cartoon for Moses and the Burning Bush*, Stanza
d'Eliodoro; Naples, Galleria Nazionale

209. PERUZZI *Moses and the Burning Bush*, Stanza d'Eliodoro, ceiling

210. PERUZZI *Jacob's Dream*, Stanza d'Eliodoro, ceiling

212. PERUZZI *Holy Family in a Landscape*, London, Pouncey
Collection

211. PERUZZI *Adoration of the Child*, Rome, S. Rocco

157

213. RAPHAEL *Stanza d'Eliodoro*, Rome, Vatican

214. RAPHAEL *Mass of Bolsena*, Stanza d'Eliodoro

215. RAPHAEL *Mass of Bolsena* (detail)

216. RAPHAEL *Mass of Bolsena* (detail), *Swiss Guards*

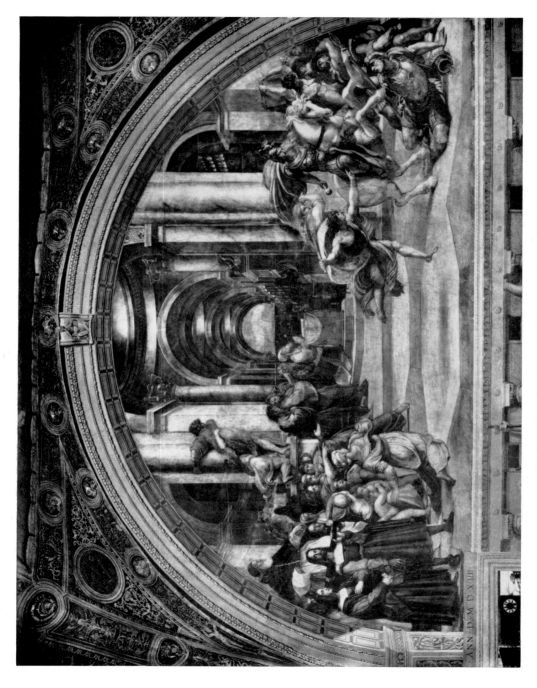

217. RAPHAEL *Expulsion of Heliodorus*, Stanza d'Eliodoro

218. RAPHAEL *Expulsion of Heliodorus* (detail)

163

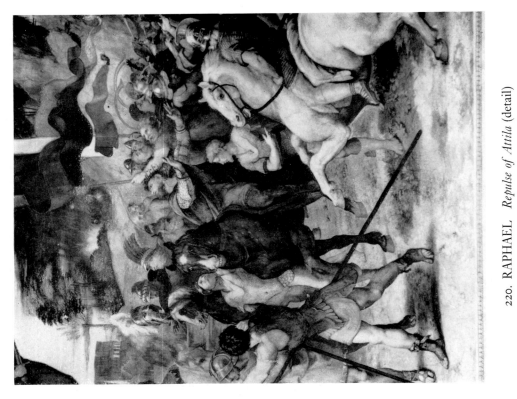

220. RAPHAEL *Repulse of Attila* (detail)

219. RAPHAEL *Expulsion of Heliodorus* (detail)

221. RAPHAEL, *Repulse of Attila*, Stanza d'Eliodoro

222. RAPHAEL *Liberation of Peter*, Stanza d'Eliodoro

223. RAPHAEL *Liberation of Peter* (detail)

224. RAPHAEL *Liberation of Peter* (detail)

226. GIULIO *Basamento* (detail; repainted), Stanza d'Eliodoro

225. RAPHAEL ASSISTANT *Grotesque Decoration*, Stanza d'Eliodoro

227. RAPHAEL *Study for a Resurrection*, Bayonne, Musée Bonnat

228. RAPHAEL *Study for a Resurrection*, Windsor,
Royal Library

229. RAPHAEL *Study for a Resurrection*, Oxford, Ashmolean

230. RAPHAEL *Galatea*, Rome, Villa Farnesina

231. RAPHAEL ASSISTANT *Prophets*, Rome, S.M. della Pace, Cappella Chigi

232. RAPHAEL *Sibyls*, S.M. della Pace, Cappella Chigi

233. RAPHAEL   *Sibyls* (detail), S.M. della Pace

234. RAPHAEL *Sibyls* (detail), S.M. della Pace

235. RAPHAEL *Sistine Madonna*, Dresden, Gallery

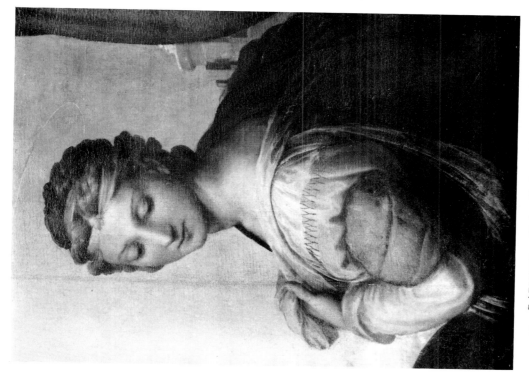

237. RAPHAEL *Sistine Madonna* (detail), *St. Barbara*

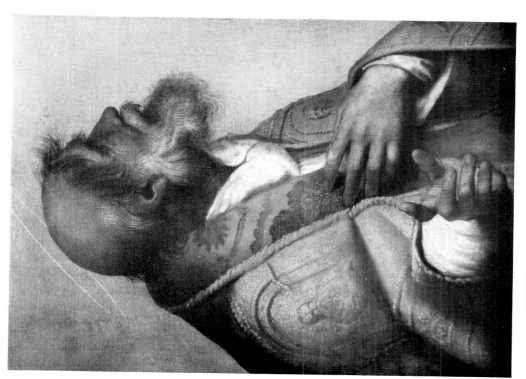

236. RAPHAEL *Sistine Madonna* (detail), *St. Sixtus*

177

239. RAPHAEL   *Study for Madonna dell'Impannata*, Windsor, Royal Library

238. RAPHAEL [with Penni and Giulio]   *Madonna of the Fish*, Madrid, Prado

240. RAPHAEL [with Giulio] *Madonna dell'Impannata*, Florence, Pitti

241. RAPHAEL *St. Cecilia Altar*, Bologna, Pinacoteca

243. RAPHAEL *St. Cecilia Altar* (detail)

242. RAPHAEL *St. Cecilia Altar* (detail)

245. RAPHAEL ASSISTANT *Tommaso Inghirami*,
Florence, Pitti

244. RAPHAEL, *Tommaso Inghirami* ("Il Fedra"), Boston,
Gardner Museum

182

246. RAPHAEL [or assistant] *Giuliano de'Medici*, New York, Metropolitan Museum

247. RAPHAEL *La Donna Velata*, Florence, Pitti

248. RAPHAEL *Madonna della Sedia*, Florence, Pitti

249. RAPHAEL *Madonna della Sedia* (detail)

250. LEONARDO [and assistant ?]
St. John Baptist, Paris, Louvre

251. LEONARDO *Cataclysm*, Windsor, Royal Library

IV

THE MATURATION OF CLASSICAL STYLE IN FLORENCE (c. 1508-c. 1514)

252. FRA BARTOLOMMEO   *Holy Family*, London, National Gallery 3914

253. FRA BARTOLOMMEO *God the Father with Sts. Mary Magdalen and Catherine of Siena,*
Lucca, Pinacoteca

254. FRA BARTOLOMMEO [with Albertinelli] *Madonna with Six Saints*, Florence, S. Marco

255. FRA BARTOLOMMEO *Madonna with Sts. Stephen and John Baptist*, Lucca, Cathedral

256. ALBERTINELLI *Madonna with Four Saints*, Florence, Academy

258. ALBERTINELLI *Study for a Trinity*, Florence, Uffizi

257. ALBERTINELLI *Trinity*, Florence, Academy

194

259. ALBERTINELLI *Annunciation*, Florence, Academy

260. FRA BARTOLOMMEO *Marriage of St. Catherine*, Paris, Louvre

261. FRA BARTOLOMMEO [with Albertinelli] *Virgin in Glory with Saints*, Besançon, Cathedral

262. ALBERTINELLI *Coronation of the Virgin* (fragment; former crown-piece of 261), Stuttgart, Gallery

263. FRA BARTOLOMMEO *St. Anne Altar*, Florence, Museo di S. Marco

264. FRA BARTOLOMMEO [with assistants] *The Marriage of St. Catherine* (The *Pitti Pala*), Florence, Academy

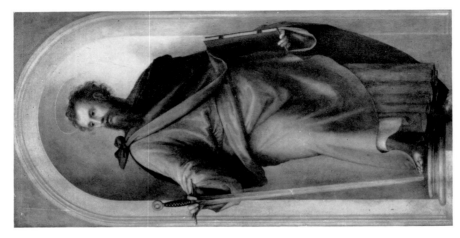

266. FRA BARTOLOMMEO   *St. Paul*,
Rome, Vatican Museum

265.   FRA BARTOLOMMEO [with
Raphael]   *St. Peter*,
Rome, Vatican Museum

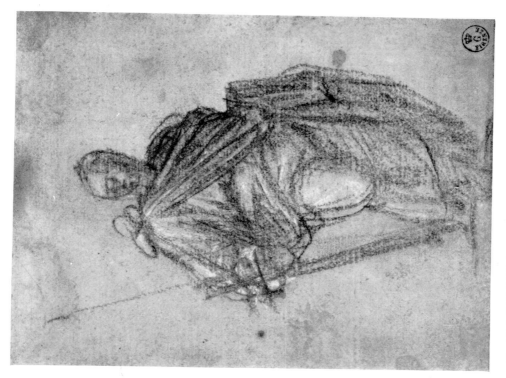

268. FRA BARTOLOMMEO *Study for St. Paul*, Florence, Uffizi

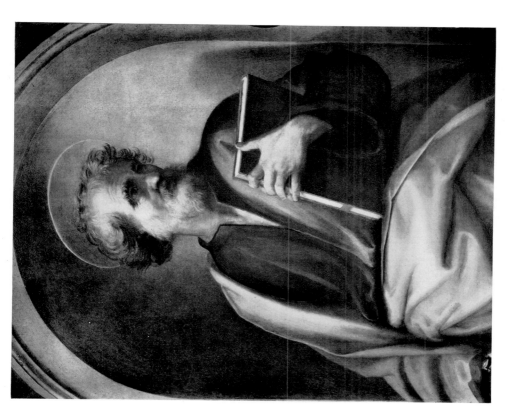

267. FRA BARTOLOMMEO [with Raphael] *St. Peter* (detail)

270. BUGIARDINI *Portrait of a Young Woman*, Paris, Musée
Jacquemart–André

269. BUGIARDINI *La Monaca*, Florence, Pitti

202

272. BUGIARDINI *Madonna and Child with St. John* (formerly ?)
New York, C. H. Holmes Collection

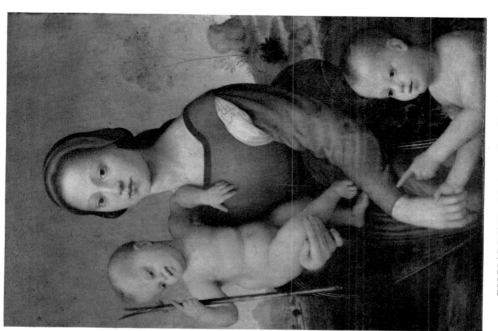

271. BUGIARDINI *Madonna Standing in a Landscape*
(sold London, 1946)

203

273. BUGIARDINI   *Madonna and Child with St. John* (formerly) London, Agnew

274. BUGIARDINI   *Madonna del Latte*, Florence, Uffizi

275. BUGIARDINI *Ariadne* (?), Venice, Ca' d'Oro

276. BUGIARDINI *Leda*, Milan, Treccani Collection

277. RIDOLFO GHIRLANDAIO
Portrait of a Lady, Florence, Pitti

278. RIDOLFO GHIRLANDAIO
Adoration of the Child
(destroyed; formerly Berlin,
Museums)

279. RIDOLFO GHIRLANDAIO *Adoration of the Shepherds*, Budapest, Museum

280. RIDOLFO GHIRLANDAIO *Nativity with Six Saints*, New York, Metropolitan Museum

281. RIDOLFO GHIRLANDAIO [shop assistant]
Adoration of the Shepherds (formerly) London,
Henry Harris Collection

282. RIDOLFO GHIRLANDAIO *Madonna della
Cintola*, Prato, Cathedral

283. RIDOLFO GHIRLANDAIO   *Portrait of a Goldsmith*, Florence, Pitti

284. RIDOLFO GHIRLANDAIO [with Andrea di Cosimo] *Decoration of Cappella dei Priori, Florence, Palazzo Vecchio*

285. RIDOLFO GHIRLANDAIO [with Andrea di Cosimo] *Decoration of Cappella dei Priori*

287. GRANACCI *Madonna della Cintola*, Sarasota, Ringling Museum

286. GRANACCI *Madonna with Two Saints*, Villamagna (near Florence), S. Donnino

212

289. GRANACCI *Pietà*, Quintole, S. Pietro

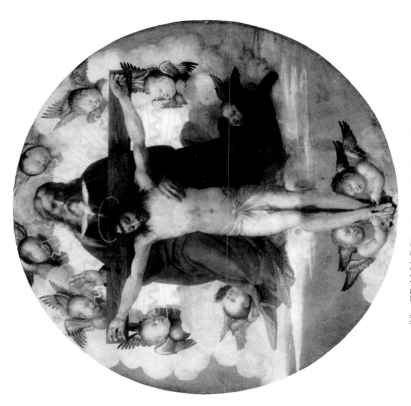

288. GRANACCI *Trinity*, Berlin, Museums

290. GRANACCI *Madonna in Glory with Four Saints*, Florence, Academy

291. GRANACCI *Holy Family with St. John*, Florence, Pitti

292. PIERO DI COSIMO [with assistants] *Doctrine of the Immaculate Conception*, Fiesole, S. Francesco

293. PIERO DI COSIMO *Legend of Prometheus*, Munich, Pinakothek

294. PIERO DI COSIMO *Legend of Prometheus*, Strasbourg, Museum

295. PIERO DI COSIMO *Adoration of the Child*, Rome, Borghese

296. ANDREA DEL SARTO *Pietà*, Rome, Borghese

298. ANDREA DEL SARTO *Baptism of Christ*, Florence, Scalzo

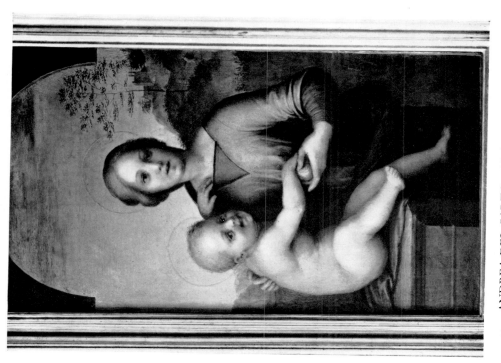

297. ANDREA DEL SARTO *Madonna*, Rome, Galleria
Nazionale

300. ANDREA DEL SARTO *Burial of St. Philip*, Florence, SS. Annunziata

299. ANDREA DEL SARTO *Healing of the Obsessed Girl*, Florence, SS. Annunziata

302. ANDREA DEL SARTO *Punishment of the Gamblers*, Florence,
SS. Annunziata

301. ANDREA DEL SARTO *Healing by St. Philip's Relics*, Florence,
SS. Annunziata

304. ANDREA DEL SARTO *Noli Me Tangere*, Florence, Uffizi

303. ANDREA DEL SARTO *Clothing of the Leper*, Florence, SS. Annunziata

306. FRANCIABIGIO *Adoration of the Shepherds*, Florence, Museo di S. Marco

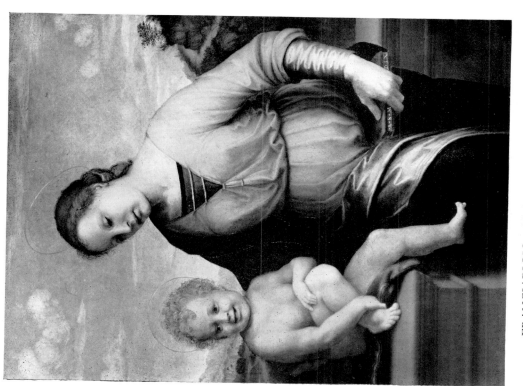

305. FRANCIABIGIO *Madonna*, Rome, Galleria Nazionale

307. FRANCIABIGIO *Last Supper*, Florence, S.M. dei Candeli

308. ANDREA DEL SARTO   *Adoration of the Magi*, Florence, SS. Annunziata

309. ANDREA DEL SARTO *Annunciation*, Florence, Pitti

310. ANDREA DEL SARTO [with Puligo ?] *Marriage of St. Catherine*, Dresden, Gallery

311. ANDREA DEL SARTO *Birth of the Virgin*, Florence, SS. Annunziata

312. ANDREA DEL SARTO *Birth of the Virgin* (detail)

313. ANDREA DEL SARTO *Birth of the Virgin* (detail)

314. FRANCIABIGIO *Marriage of the Virgin*, Florence, SS. Annunziata

315. FRANCIABIGIO *Last Supper*, Florence, Convento della Calza

316. FRANCIABIGIO *Last Supper* (detail)

320.   ANDREA DEL SARTO [with Puligo ?]   *Madonna with the*
Infant St. John, Rome, Borghese 336

319.   PULIGO   *Madonna and Child with St. John*, Rome,
Palazzo Venezia

235

321. ANDREA DEL SARTO [with Puligo?] *Tobias Altar*, Vienna, Kunsthistorisches Museum

322. PULIGO *Madonna with St. John Approaching in a Landscape*, Rome, Borghese 338

323. PONTORMO *Ospedale di S. Matteo*, Florence, Academy

324. PONTORMO *Madonna with Four Saints* (altar fresco from S. Ruffillo), Florence, SS. Annunziata

326. ROSSO *Madonna in a Landscape*. Arezzo, Museum (from Uffizi Deposit 8309)

325. ROSSO *Madonna and Child*, New York, Finch College, Kress Collection 485

328. BERRUGUETE *Madonna and Elizabeth with the Two Holy
Children*, Rome, Borghese 335

327. ROSSO *Holy Family*, Rome, Borghese

330. [Anon.] *Madonna* (formerly) Milan, Crespi Collection

329. BERRUGUETE *Madonna*, Milan, Saibene Collection

241

331. FILIPPINO LIPPI, BERRUGUETE [and others] *Coronation of the Virgin*, Paris, Louvre

332. MANCHESTER MASTER   *Madonna and Child with St. John,*
Vienna, Academy

333. MANCHESTER MASTER   *Virgin Reading with the
Christ Child and St. John,* New York, Kress Collection

335. MANCHESTER MASTER *Madonna*, Baden bei Zurich, Private
Collection

334. MANCHESTER MASTER *Pietà*, Rome, Galleria Nazionale

244

337. MANCHESTER MASTER *Madonna*, Florence, Art Market

336. MANCHESTER MASTER *Madonna with St. John and Four Angels*, London, National Gallery

245

338. MICHELANGELO [with the Manchester Master] *Entombment*, London National Gallery

V

CLIMAX, CRISIS, AND DISSOLUTION OF THE CLASSICAL STYLE IN ROME

(c. 1514 - c. 1520)

339. RAPHAEL *Acts of the Apostles* (tapestries), Rome, Vatican Museum
(in order of arrangement in the Sistine Chapel)

340. RAPHAEL   *The Stoning of Stephen* (tapestry)

341. RAPHAEL   *The Conversion of Paul* (tapestry)

342. RAPHAEL *Miraculous Draught of Fishes* (tapestry)

343. RAPHAEL *Pasce Oves* (tapestry)

251

PIVS·VII·P·M·
CONCLAVIA·HAEC·
AVLAEIS·INTEXTIS·EX·ARCHETYPIS·VRBINATIS·
GENTIVM·ADMIRATIONI·ARTIVM·COMMODITATI·
EXPLICANDIS·ET·SERVANDIS·
APTIVS·DISPOSVIT·EXORNAVITVE·
CVR·B·NARO·S·P·A·PRÆFECTO·

344. RAPHAEL   *Blinding of Elymas* (tapestry fragment)

345. RAPHAEL   *Paul at Lystra* (tapestry)

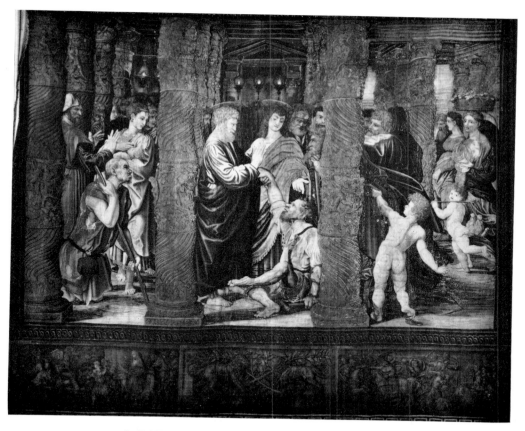

346. RAPHAEL   *Healing at the Golden Gate* (tapestry)

347. RAPHAEL   *Death of Ananias* (tapestry)

348. RAPHAEL *Paul Preaching at Athens* (tapestry)

349. RAPHAEL *Study for the Pasce Oves*, Windsor, Royal Library

350. RAPHAEL *Study for the Christ of the Pasce Oves*, Paris, Louvre

351. RAPHAEL *Study for the Paul at Lystra*, Chatsworth

352. RAPHAEL *Study for the Blinding of Elymas*, Windsor, Royal Library

353. PENNI *Study for the Pasce Oves*, Paris, Louvre

354. PENNI *Study for Paul Preaching at Athens*, Florence, Uffizi

355. RAPHAEL. *Miraculous Draught of Fishes* (tapestry cartoon), London, Victoria and Albert Museum

356. RAPHAEL   *Miraculous Draught of Fishes* (tapestry cartoon, detail)

357. RAPHAEL   *Miraculous Draught of Fishes* (tapestry cartoon, detail)

358. RAPHAEL *Pasce Oves* (tapestry cartoon), London, Victoria and Albert Museum

261

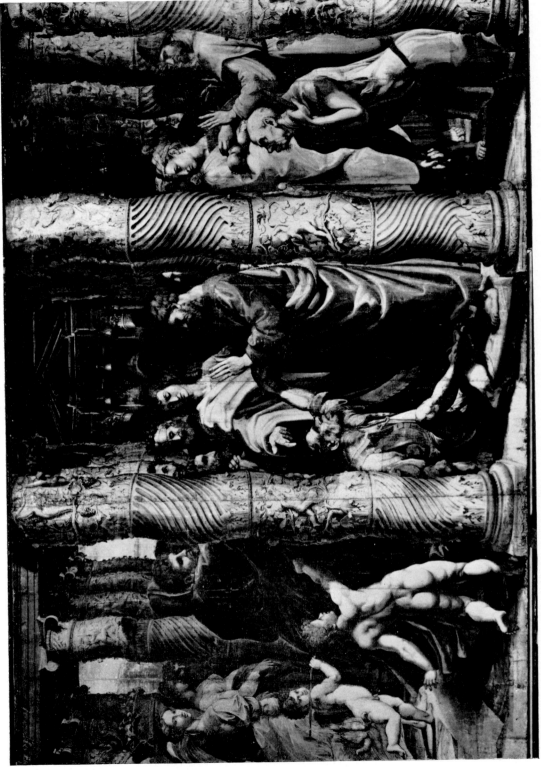

259 RAPHAEL, *Healing at the Golden Gate* (tapestry cartoon), London, Victoria and Albert Museum

361. RAPHAEL *Healing at the Golden Gate* (tapestry cartoon, detail)

360. RAPHAEL *Healing at the Golden Gate* (tapestry cartoon, detail)

362. RAPHAEL *Death of Ananias* (tapestry cartoon), London, Victoria and Albert Museum

363. RAPHAEL *Death of Ananias* (tapestry cartoon, detail)

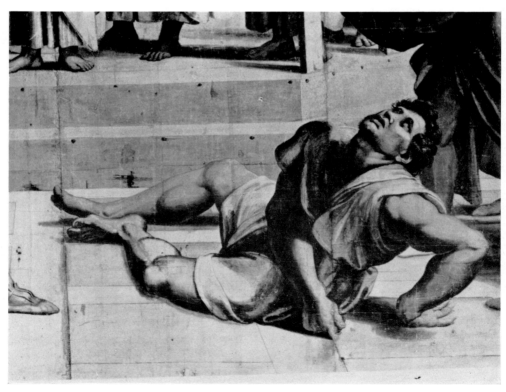

364, 365. RAPHAEL *Death of Ananias* (tapestry cartoon, details)

366. RAPHAEL [with Penni] *Blinding of Elymas* (tapestry cartoon), London, Victoria and Albert Museum

367. RAPHAEL *Paul at Lystra* (tapestry cartoon), London, Victoria and Albert Museum

368. RAPHAEL *Paul at Lystra* (tapestry cartoon, detail)

369. RAPHAEL [with Penni] *Paul Preaching at Athens* (tapestry cartoon), London, Victoria and Albert Museum

370. PENNI *Paul Preaching at Athens* (tapestry cartoon, detail)

371. RAPHAEL *Paul at Lystra* (tapestry cartoon, detail)

372. PENNI *Study for the Miraculous Draught of Fishes*, Vienna, Albertina

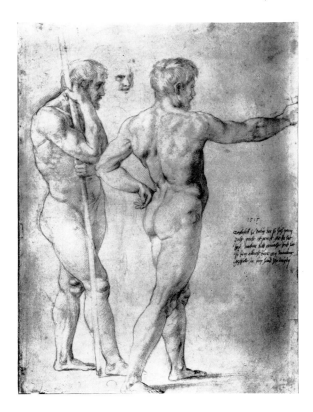

373. GIULIO [retouched by Raphael
Study for the Battle of Ostia, Vienn
Albertina

374. RAPHAEL [with Giulio] *Battle of Ostia*, Rome, Vatican, Stanza dell'Incendio

375. GIULIO *Battle of Ostia* (detail)

376. RAPHAEL [with Giulio] *Fire in the Borgo*, Rome, Vatican, Stanza dell'Incendio

377. GIULIO *Fire in the Borgo* (detail)

378, 379. GIULIO *Fire in the Borgo* (details)

380. RAPHAEL [with Penni] *Coronation of Charlemagne*, Rome, Vatican, Stanza dell'Incendio

381. PENNI   *Coronation of Charlemagne* (detail)

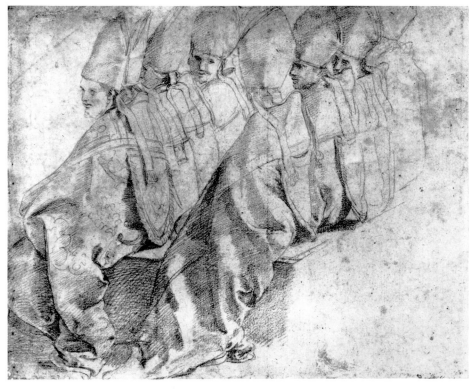

382. PENNI   *Study for the Coronation of Charlemagne*, Düsseldorf, Museum

279

383: RAPHAEL [with Penni] *Oath of Leo*, Rome, Vatican, Stanza dell'Incendio

384. PENNI *Study for the Oath of Leo*, Florence, Horne Foundation

385. GIULIO *Basamento* (detail), Rome, Vatican, Stanza dell'Incendio

386. RAPHAEL [with Alvise de Pace] *Cupola of the Cappella Chigi*, Rome, S.M. del Popolo

387, 388. RAPHAEL *Studies for the Cappella Chigi*, Oxford, Ashmolean

389. RAPHAEL [with Giovanni da Udine] *Loggetta of the Cardinal Bibbiena*, Rome, Vatican

390. RAPHAEL [with Giovanni da Udine] *Loggetta of the Cardinal Bibbiena*, Rome, Vatican

391. GIOVANNI DA UDINE [and assistants]   *Loggetta of the Cardinal Bibbiena* (detail)

392, 393. RAPHAEL [with Giovanni da Udine] *Stufetta of the Cardinal Bibbiena*, Rome, Vatican

394. TADDEO ZUCCARO [and others] *Decoration of the Sala dei Palafrenieri* (free reconstruction of Raphael), Rome, Vatican

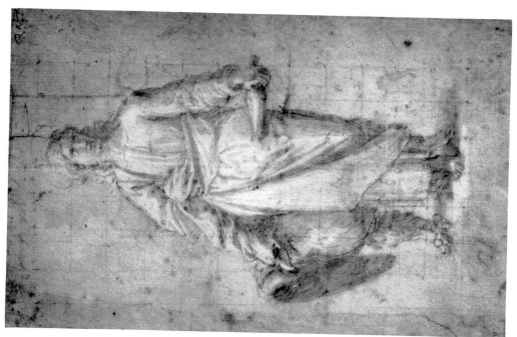

395, 396. PENNI *Studies for the Sala dei Palafrenieri*, Paris, Louvre

397. RAPHAEL [and assistants]   *Sala di Psiche*, Rome, Villa Farnesina

398. GIULIO *Three Graces*, Sala di Psiche

399. GIULIO *Venus, Ceres, and Juno*, Sala di Psiche

400. GIULIO *Jupiter and Cupid*, Sala di Psiche

401. GIULIO *Venus and Psyche*, Sala di Psiche

402. RAPHAEL *Study for Venus and Psyche*, Paris, Louvre

404. PENNI *Mercury Descending*, Sala di Psiche

403. PENNI *Venus before Jupiter*, Rome, Villa Farnesina, Sala di Psiche

406. GIOVANNI DA UDINE *Amoretto with Mythic Beasts*, Sala di Psiche

405. RAFFAELLINO DEL COLLE (?) *Venus and Cupid*, Sala di Psiche

407. RAPHAEL *Study for the Wedding Feast of Cupid and Psyche*, Windsor, Royal Library

408. PENNI *Council of the Gods*, Rome, Villa Farnesina, Sala di Psiche

409. PENNI *Wedding Feast of Cupid and Psyche*, Sala di Psiche

410. RAPHAEL [and assistants]   *Logge*, Rome, Vatican

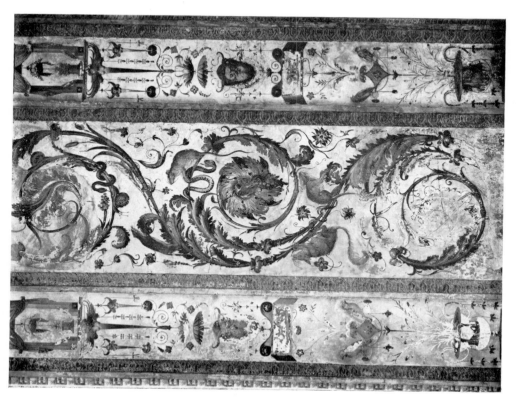

411, 412. GIOVANNI DA UDINE [and assistants] *Grotesque Decorations* (details), Rome, Vatican, Logge

413. GIOVANNI DA UDINE   *Borders from the Tapestries of the Acts of the Apostles*, Rome, Vatican Museum

414. POLIDORO *Grotesque Decorations*, Rome, Vatican, Stanza dell'Incendio

303

415. RAPHAEL [and assistants] *Logge* (first bay), Rome, Vatican

416. RAPHAEL [and assistants] *Logge* (second bay), Rome, Vatican

304

417. RAPHAEL [and assistants]   *Logge* (third bay), Rome, Vatican

418. RAPHAEL [and assistants]   *Logge* (fourth bay), Rome, Vatican

419. RAPHAEL [and assistants]   *Logge* (fifth bay), Rome, Vatican

420. RAPHAEL [and assistants]   *Logge* (sixth bay), Rome, Vatican

306

421. RAPHAEL [and assistants]   *Logge* (seventh bay), Rome, Vatican

422. GIOVANNI DA UDINE   *Lower Loggia*, Rome, Vatican, Cortile di S. Damaso

423. RAPHAEL *Baldassare Castiglione*, Paris, Louvre

425. RAPHAEL *Antonio Tebaldeo* (copy), Florence, Uffizi

424. RAPHAEL. *Antonio Tebaldeo* (from the *Parnassus* fresco), Rome, Vatican

426. RAPHAEL *Andrea Navugero and Agostino Beazzano*, Rome, Galleria Doria

428. RAPHAEL   *Cardinal Bernardo Bibbiena* (copy), Florence, Uffizi

427. GIULIO   *Bindo Altoviti*, Washington, National Gallery, Kress Collection

429. RAPHAEL *Leo X with the Cardinals Giulio de' Medici and Luigi Rossi*, Florence, Pitti

430. RAPHAEL   *Raphael and His Fencing Master*, Paris, Louvre

431. GIULIO *Giovanna d'Aragona*, Paris, Louvre

432. RAPHAEL   *Madonna della Tenda*, Munich, Pinakothek

433. RAPHAEL [with Penni] *Spasimo di Sicilia*, Madrid, Prado

435. GIULIO *Cartoon for the Holy Family of Francis I* (fragment), Melbourne, National Gallery

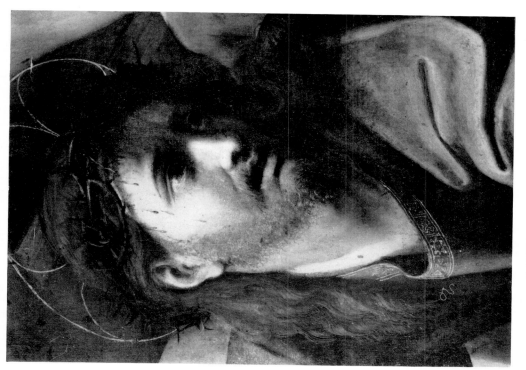

434. RAPHAEL *Spasimo di Sicilia* (detail)

436. RAPHAEL [with Giulio]   *Holy Family of Francis I*, Paris, Louvre

437. RAPHAEL [with Giulio] *St. Michael*, Paris, Louvre

438. RAPHAEL [and assistants] *Transfiguration*, Rome, Vatican Museum

439. PENNI *Transfiguration* (detail)

440. RAPHAEL [and Giulio]   *Transfiguration* (detail)

441. GIULIO *Transfiguration* (detail)

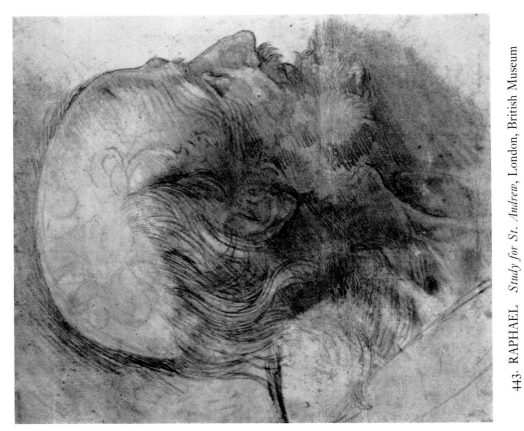

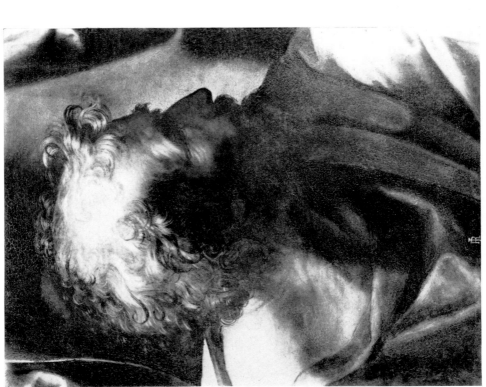

445. GIULIO (?) *Study for the Transfiguration*,
Paris, Louvre

444. RAPHAEL *Study for the Transfiguration*,
Oxford, Ashmolean

325

447. GIULIO *St. Margaret*, Paris, Louvre

446. GIULIO *Madonna Piccola Gonzaga*, Paris, Louvre

448. GIULIO *Madonna della Perla*, Madrid, Prado

450. PENNI *Madonna del Divino Amore*, Naples, Galleria Nazionale

449. PENNI *Visitation*, Madrid, Prado

452. GIULIO [with Raffaellino] *Madonna della Rosa*, Madrid, Prado

451. GIULIO [with Penni] *St. John Baptist*, Florence, Academy

329

453. GIULIO [with Raffaellino] *Madonna of the Oak*, Madrid, Prado

455. SEBASTIANO *Man in Armor*, Hartford, Atheneum

457. SEBASTIANO *Portrait of a Young Man*, Budapest, Museum

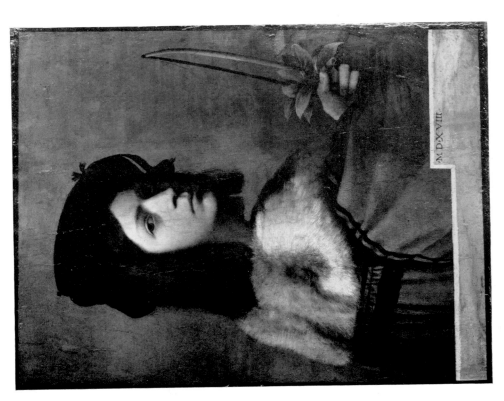

456. SEBASTIANO *Young Violinist*, Paris, Baron G. de Rothschild

458. SEBASTIANO *Cardinal Antonio Ciocchi del Monte Sansovino*, Dublin, National Gallery

459. SEBASTIANO *Verdelotti and Ubretto* (destroyed; formerly Berlin, Museums)

460. SEBASTIANO *Cardinal Bandinello Sauli and Suite*, Washington, National Gallery, Kress Collection

461. SEBASTIANO *Pietà*, Viterbo, Museum

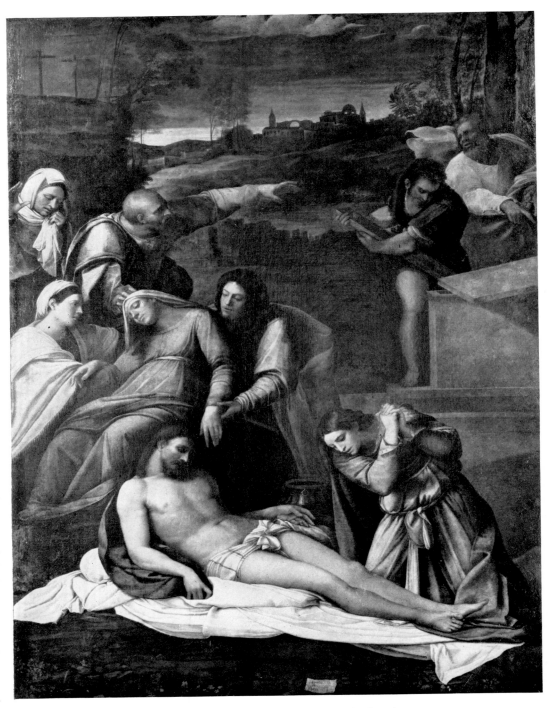

462. SEBASTIANO *Pietà*, Leningrad, Hermitage

463. SEBASTIANO   *Resurrection of Lazarus*, London, National Gallery

464. SEBASTIANO *Resurrection of Lazarus* (detail)

466. SEBASTIANO *Holy Family with St. John Baptist and Donor,*
London, National Gallery

465. SEBASTIANO *Resurrection of Lazarus* (detail)

339

467. SEBASTIANO *Cappella Borgherini*, Rome, S. Pietro in Montorio

468. SEBASTIANO *Two Prophets*, Cappella Borgherini

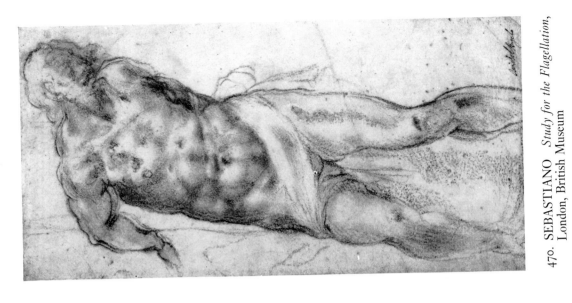

470. SEBASTIANO *Study for the Flagellation*, London, British Museum

469. SEBASTIANO *Flagellation*, Cappella Borgherini

342

472. SEBASTIANO *Study for the Flagellation*, London, British Museum

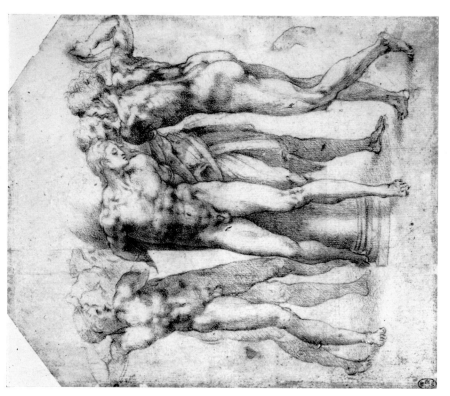

471. MICHELANGELO *Modello for the Flagellation* (copy),
Windsor, Royal Library

343

473. SEBASTIANO *Transfiguration*, Cappella Borgherini

344

474. SEBASTIANO *Visitation*, Paris, Louvre

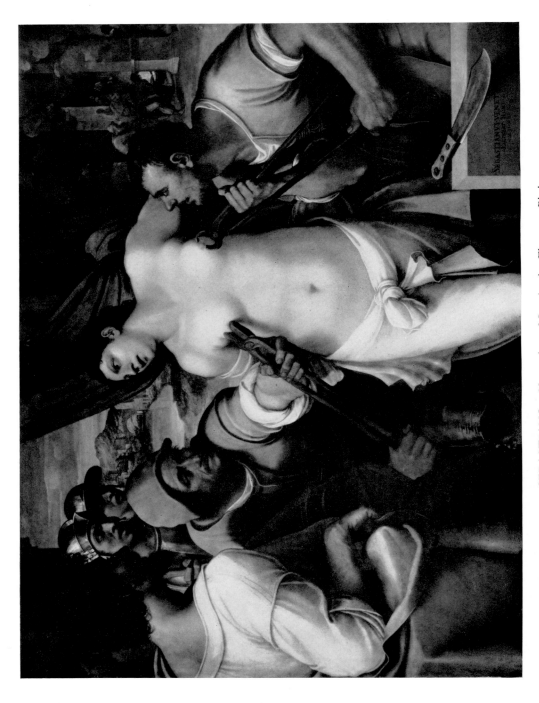

475. SEBASTIANO *Martyrdom of St. Agatha*, Florence, Pitti

476. SEBASTIANO *Study for St. Agatha*, Paris, Louvre

477. VIRGILIO ROMANO *House in Vicolo del Campanile, Rome*

478. PERUZZI *Sala delle Prospettive*, Rome, Villa Farnesina

479. PERUZZI   *Sala delle Prospettive*, Rome, Villa Farnesina

480. PERUZZI   *Sala delle Prospettive* (detail)

481. PERUZZI   *Death of Adonis*, Sala delle Prospettive

482. PERUZZI   *Procession of Bacchus*, Sala delle Prospettive

351

483. PERUZZI *Ducalion and Pyrrha,* Sala delle Prospettive

485. PERUZZI *Apollo*, Sala delle Prospettive

484. PERUZZI *Venus and Cupid*, Sala delle Prospettive

353

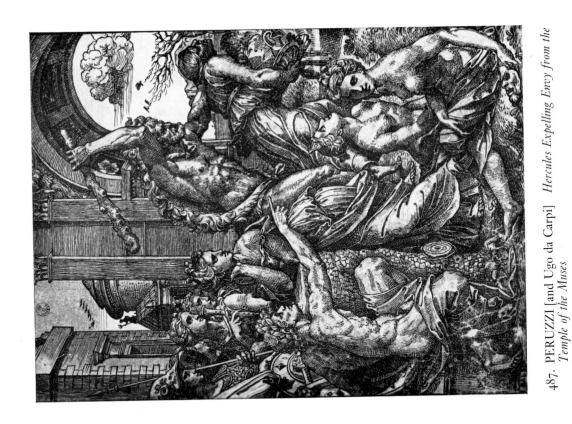

487. PERUZZI [and Ugo da Carpi] *Hercules Expelling Envy from the Temple of the Muses*

486. PERUZZI (?) [and Marcantonio] *Quos Ego*

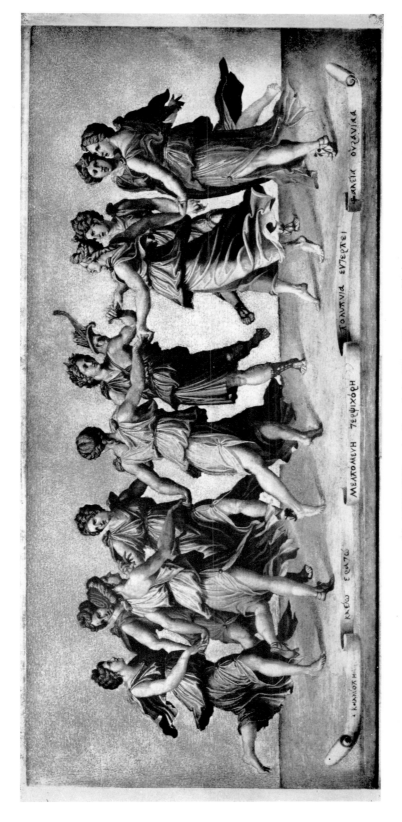

488. PERUZZI *Apollo and the Muses*, Florence, Pitti

489. PERUZZI *Country Festival*, Florence, Uffizi

356

490. PERUZZI *Ponzetti Chapel* (vault frescoes), Rome, S.M. della Pace

491. PERUZZI *Ponzetti Chapel* (vault frescoes, detail)

492. PERUZZI *Ponzetti Chapel* (altar fresco)

493. PERUZZI *Portrait of a Carmelite*, Rome, Art Market

494. PERUZZI *Presentation of the Virgin*, Rome, S.M. della Pace

495· PERUZZI [and assistants] *Decoration in the Palazzo della Cancelleria, Rome*

496. PERUZZI [and assistants] *Decoration in the Palazzo della Cancelleria, Rome*

497. PERUZZI *Joseph put into the Well*, Cancelleria

498. PERUZZI *Meeting of Solomon and Sheba*, Cancelleria

499. PENNI (?)   *Separation of Light and Darkness*, Rome, Vatican, Logge

500. GIULIO   *Expulsion*, Logge

365

501. GIULIO   *God Appearing to Isaac*, Logge

502. GIULIO   *Isaac and Rebecca*, Logge

503. GIULIO [with Polidoro ?] *Jacob and Rachel*, Logge

504. GIULIO (?) [with Perino] *Flight of Jacob*, Logge

505. GIULIO (?) *Crossing of the Red Sea*, Logge

506. GIULIO (?) [with Polidoro] *Moses Striking Water from the Rock*, Logge

507. GIULIO *Moses Receiving the Tablets of the Law*, Logge

508. GIULIO (?) *Adoration of the Golden Calf*, Logge

369

509. PERINO *Fall of Jericho*, Logge

510. PERINO *Joshua Stays the Sun*, Logge

511. PERINO   *Division of the Lands*, Logge

512. PERINO   *David and Goliath*, Logge

513. PERINO *David and Bathsheba*, Logge

514. PELLEGRINO (?) *Judgment of Solomon*, Logge

515. POLIDORO *Meeting of Solomon and Sheba*, Logge

516. POLIDORO *Building of the Temple*, Logge

517. PERINO *Adoration of the Shepherds*, Logge

518. PERINO *Adoration of the Kings*, Logge

374

519. PERINO *Baptism of Christ*, Logge

520. PERINO *Last Supper*, Logge

375

521. PENNI *Study for Separation of Light and Darkness*, London, British Museum

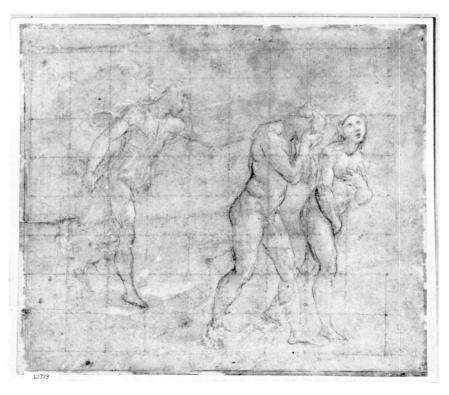

522. PENNI *Study for Expulsion*, Windsor, Royal Library

523. PENNI *Study for Jacob's Dream*, London, British Museum

524. PENNI *Study for Adoration of the Golden Calf*, Florence, Uffizi

525. PERINO *Study for Division of the Lands*, Windsor, Royal Library

526. PERINO *Lamentation over Christ*, Paris, Louvre

527. PERINO   *Pietà*, Rome, Sto. Stefano del Cacco

528. PERINO *Adoration of the Child*, Rome, Borghese 464

V I

CLIMAX AND CRISIS IN FLORENCE AND THE GENERATION OF FLORENTINE MANNERISM (c. 1514-1520)

529. FRA BARTOLOMMEO *Virgin and Child*, Florence, Convent of S. Marco

531. FRA BARTOLOMMEO *Study for the Madonna della Misericordia,*
Florence, Uffizi

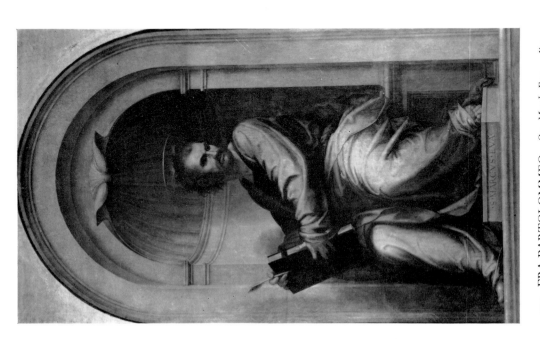

530. FRA BARTOLOMMEO *St. Mark Evangelist,*
Florence, Pitti

532. FRA BARTOLOMMEO *Madonna della Misericordia*, Lucca, Pinacoteca

533. FRA BARTOLOMMEO *Annunciation*, Le Caldine, Convento della Maddalena

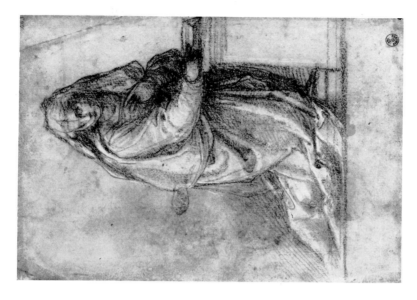

534. FRA BARTOLOMMEO *Study for the Galline Annunciation*, Florence, Uffizi

535. FRA BARTOLOMMEO *Annunciation Altar*, Paris, Louvre

536. FRA BARTOLOMMEO *Salvator Mundi*, Florence, Pitti

538. FRA BARTOLOMMEO *Study for Salvator Mundi,*
Amsterdam, Rijksmuseum

537. FRA BARTOLOMMEO *Studies for the Salvator Mundi and
Other Projects,* Florence, Uffizi

539. FRA BARTOLOMMEO *Presentation in the Temple*, Vienna, Kunsthistorisches Museum

540. FRA BARTOLOMMEO *Isaiah*, Florence, Academy

541. FRA BARTOLOMMEO *Job*, Florence, Academy

543. FRA BARTOLOMMEO *Study for the Assumption,* Munich, Graphische Sammlung

542. FRA BARTOLOMMEO [with Fra Paolino] *Assumption of the Virgin,* Naples, Galleria Nazionale

393

544. FRA BARTOLOMMEO *Holy Family*, Rome, Galleria Nazionale

545. FRA BARTOLOMMEO *Madonna and Child with Elizabeth and John*, London, Kenwood, Iveagh Bequest

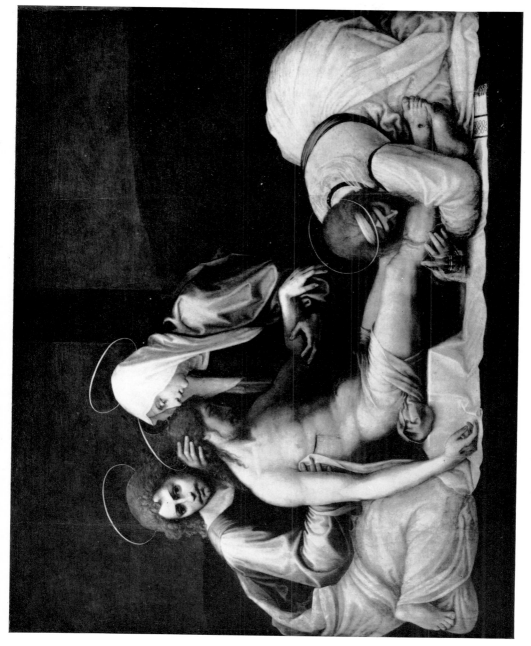

546. FRA BARTOLOMMEO [with Bugiardini] *Pietà*, Florence, Pitti

547. FRA BARTOLOMMEO *Noli Me Tangere*, Le Caldine, Convento della Maddalena

549. FRA PAOLINO *Holy Family with St. John and Angels*, Rome, Galleria Doria

548. FRA PAOLINO *Crucifixion*, Siena, Sto. Spirito

550. FRA PAOLINO *Pietà*, Florence, Museo di S. Marco

551. ANDREA DEL SARTO *Scenes from the Life of St. John Baptist*, Florence, Scalzo

552. ANDREA DEL SARTO *Preaching of St. John Baptist*, Florence, Scalzo

553. ANDREA DEL SARTO *Justice*, Florence, Scalzo

554. ANDREA DEL SARTO *Charity*, Florence, Scalzo

555. ANDREA DEL SARTO *Chiaroscuro Panel* (from the Leo X Festival Decoration ?), Florence, Uffizi

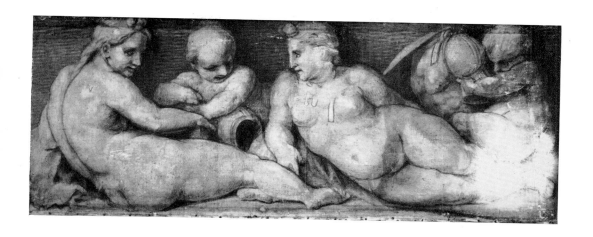

556, 557. ANDREA DEL SARTO *Chiaroscuro Panels* (from the Leo X Festival Decoration ?), Florence, Uffizi

558. ANDREA DEL SARTO *Holy Family with St. Catherine*, Leningrad, Hermitage

560. ANDREA DEL SARTO   *Study for the Pietà*, Florence, Uffizi

559. A. VENEZIANO [after Andrea del Sarto]   *Pietà*

405

561. ANDREA DEL SARTO *Redeemer*, Florence, SS. Annunziata

562. ANDREA DEL SARTO *Holy Family*, Paris, Louvre 1515

563. ANDREA DEL SARTO *Baptism of the Multitude*, Florence, Scalzo

564. ANDREA DEL SARTO *Capture of St. John*, Florence, Scalzo

565. ANDREA DEL SARTO *Madonna of the Harpies*, Florence, Uffizi

566. ANDREA DEL SARTO *Disputation on the Trinity*, Florence, Pitti

567. ANDREA DEL SARTO
Portrait of a Sculptor (?),
London, National Gallery

568. ANDREA DEL SARTO
*Study for Portrait of a
Sculptor*, Florence, Uffizi

569. ANDREA DEL SARTO   *Caritas*, Paris, Louvre

570. ANDREA DEL SARTO   *Madonna and Child with St. John*, Rome, Borghese 334

571. ANDREA DEL SARTO   *Madonna with St. John and Angels* (?), London, Wallace Collection

572. ANDREA DEL SARTO *Pietà*, Vienna, Kunsthistorisches Museum

573. ANDREA DEL SARTO *Tribute to Caesar* (in its original dimensions), Poggio a Cajano

574. FRANCIABIGIO *Annunciation*, Turin, Galleria Sabauda

575. FRANCIABIGIO *Angel*, Florence, Sto. Spirito

576. FRANCIABIGIO   *St. Job Altar*, Florence, Uffizi

577. FRANCIABIGIO *Meeting of Christ and St. John Baptist*, Florence, Scalzo

578. FRANCIABIGIO *Madonna and Child with St. John*, Vienna, Kunsthistorisches Museum 208

420

579. FRANCIABIGIO *Benediction of St. John by Zachary*, Florence, Scalzo

580. FRANCIABIGIO
Leda, Brussels, Museum

581. FRANCIABIGIO *Madonna*, Bologna, Pinacoteca 294

582. FRANCIABIGIO *Triumph of Caesar* (in its original dimensions), Poggio a Cajano

584. FRANCIABIGIO *Portrait of Caradosso*, London, Art Market

583. FRANCIABIGIO *Self-Portrait*, New York, Hunter College, ex Kress Collection

586. FRANCIABIGIO *Portrait of a Fattore*, Hampton Court

585. FRANCIABIGIO *Portrait of a Man*, Vienna, Liechtenstein Collection

425

587a. BUGIARDINI *Temptation in the Garden of Eden*, New York, Private Collection

588. BUGIARDINI
St. Sebastian, New York,
Kress Collection

587b. BUGIARDINI *Temptation in the Garden of Eden*, New York, Private Collection

589. BUGIARDINI
*Madonna and Child with the
Infant St. John*, Dunblane,
Stirling Collection

590. BUGIARDINI *Madonna and Child with the Infant St. John*, Florence, Uffizi

591. BUGIARDINI *Madonna and Child with the Infant St. John*, Allentown (Pennsylvania) Museum, Kress Collection

592. RIDOLFO GHIRLANDAIO *Coronation of the Virgin*, Florence, S.M. Novella, Cappella del Papa

593. RIDOLFO GHIRLANDAIO *Resuscitation of a Youth by St. Zenobius,*
Florence, Academy

594. RIDOLFO GHIRLANDAIO *Translation of the Body of St. Zenobius*, Florence, Academy

595. RIDOLFO GHIRLANDAIO   *Madonna with Six Saints*, Pistoia, Museum

597. RIDOLFO GHIRLANDAIO *Portrait of a Man*, Florence, Galleria Corsini

596. RIDOLFO GHIRLANDAIO *Girolamo Benivieni* (?), London, National Gallery

598. RIDOLFO GHIRLANDAIO
Portrait of a Man, Florence,
Torrigiani Collection

599. RIDOLFO GHIRLANDAIO *Pietà*, Colle di Val d'Elsa, S. Agostino

600. GRANACCI *Madonna with Sts. Francis and Zenobius*, Florence, Academy

602. GRANACCI *Madonna and Child*, San Francisco, Palace of
the Legion of Honor

601. GRANACCI *Holy Family*, Boughton House,
Duke of Buccleuch

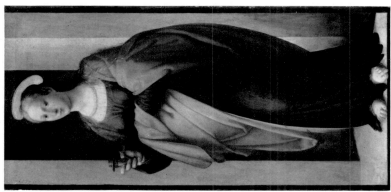

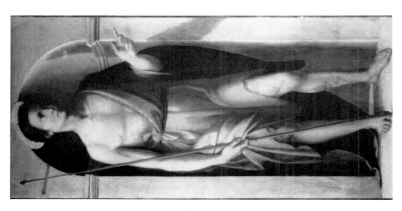

603. GRANACCI *Sts. John, Apollonia, Mary Magdalen, and Jerome* (from the *Apollonia Altar*), Munich, Pinakothek

437

604. GRANACCI *Predella Panel* (from the *Appollonia Altar*), Florence, Academy

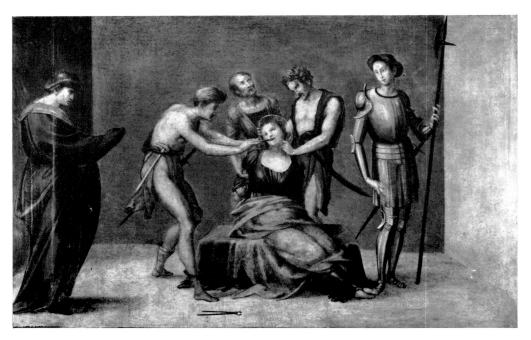

605. GRANACCI *Predella Panel* (from the *Apollonia Altar*), Florence, Academy

606. GRANACCI *Predella Panel* (from the *Apollonia Altar*), Florence, Academy

607. GRANACCI *Entry of Charles VIII into Florence*, Florence, Museo Mediceo

608. GRANACCI *Joseph Presents His Father to Pharaoh*, Florence, Uffizi

609. GRANACCI *Arrest of Joseph*, Florence, Uffizi

610. GRANACCI *Madonna with St. John*, (formerly) Munich, A. S. Drey

611. GRANACCI *Madonna with Four Saints*, Montemurlo, Pieve

612. SOGLIANI *Madonna with St. John*, Baltimore, Walters Art Gallery

613. SOGLIANI *Madonna with St. John*,
Brussels, Museum

614. SOGLIANI *Madonna with St. John*,
Turin, Galleria Sabauda

615. SOGLIANI *S. Acasio Altar*,
Florence, S. Lorenzo

616. SOGLIANI *S. Brigitta Altar*, Florence, Academy

617. PULIGO [on Sarto's cartoon]
Holy Family, London, National
Gallery

618. ANDREA [with Puligo] *Story of Joseph* (1), Florence, Pitti 87

619. ANDREA [with Puligo] *Story of Joseph* (2), Florence, Pitti 88

621. PULIGO *Madonna with St. John and Angels*, Florence, Galleria Corsini

620. PULIGO *Madonna with St. John*, Florence, Pitti 242

622. PULIGO *Adoration of the Kings* (formerly) Milan, Crespi Collection

624. PULIGO *Preaching of St. John Baptist* (formerly) London, Henry Harris Collection

623. PULIGO *Deposition*, Venice, Seminario

625. PULIGO *History of Joseph*, Rome, Borghese 463

626. PULIGO   *Apollo and Daphne*, Florence, Galleria Corsini

627. BACCHIACCA   *Deposition*, Bassano, Museo Civico

628. BACCHIACCA *Adam and Eve*, Philadelphia Museum, Johnson Collection

629. BACCHIACCA *Story of Joseph*, London, National Gallery 1218

630. BACCHIACCA *Story of Joseph*, Rome, Borghese

631. BACCHIACCA *Story of Joseph*, London, National Gallery 1219

632. BACCHIACCA *Story of Joseph*, Rome, Borghese

633. BACCHIACCA *Deposition*, Florence, Uffizi

635. BACCHIACCA *Leda*, Rotterdam, Boymans Museum, van Beuningen Collection

634. BACCHIACCA *Creation of Eve*, Stockholm, Private Collection

636, 637. BACCHIACCA   *Predella Panels* (from the *S. Acasio Altar*), Florence, Uffizi

638. BACCHIACCA *Legend of the Dead King*, Dresden, Gallery

639. PONTORMO *Visitation*, Florence, SS. Annunziata

640. PONTORMO *Visitation* (detail)

641. PONTORMO *Cappella del Papa* (vault), Florence, S.M. Novella

642. PONTORMO St. Veronica, Florence, S.M. Novella, Cappella del Papa

643. PONTORMO *Joseph Revealing Himself to His Brothers*, Henfield, Lady Salmond

645. PONTORMO *The Butler Restored and the Baker Led to Execution,* Henfield, Lady Salmond

644. PONTORMO *Joseph Sold to Potiphar,* Henfield, Lady Salmond

646. PONTORMO *Madonna and Saints*, Florence, S. Michele Visdomini

647. PONTORMO *Pietà* (predella for the Visdomini Altar), Dublin, National Gallery

648, 649. PONTORMO *St. Lawrence ; St. Francis* (portions of predella), Dublin, National Gallery

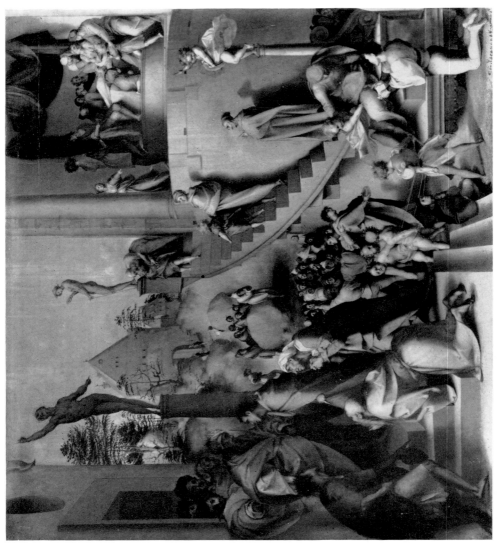

650. PONTORMO *Joseph in Egypt*, London, National Gallery

651. PONTORMO   *Cosimo de' Medici*, Florence, Uffizi

653. PONTORMO *Portrait of a Musician* (Francesco dell' Aiolle?)
Florence, Uffizi

652. PONTORMO *Study for a Portrait of Piero de' Medici*, Rome,
Galleria Corsini

654. PONTORMO *Study for St. John Evangelist*, Florence, Uffizi

655. PONTORMO *St. John Evangelist*, Empoli, Collegiata

656. PONTORMO *St. Michael*, Empoli, Collegiata

473

657. PONTORMO *Study for a Pietà*, Florence, Uffizi

658. PONTORMO *St. Anthony Abbot*, Florence, Uffizi

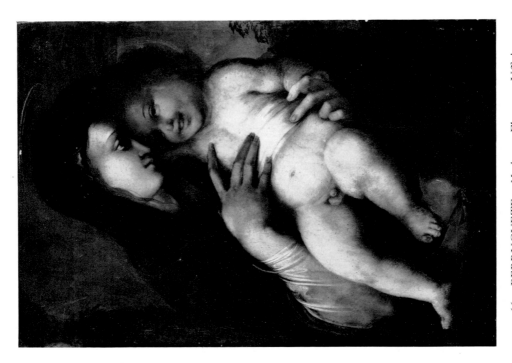

660. BERRUGUETE   *Madonna*, Florence, Uffizi

659. BERRUGUETE   *Salome*, Florence, Uffizi

476

661. BERRUGUETE *Madonna with St. John*, Florence, Palazzo Vecchio, Loeser Collection

662. ROSSO *Madonna in Glory*, Leningrad, Hermitage

478

663. ROSSO *Portrait of a Young Man*, Berlin, Museums

664. ROSSO *Assumption*, Florence, SS. Annunziata

665. ROSSO *Assumption* (detail)

666. ROSSO *Momento Mori*, Florence, Uffizi

667. ROSSO *Madonna and Saints* (*S.M.Nuova Altar*), Florence, Uffizi

668. ROSSO *S.M. Nuova Altar* (detail)

V I I

EPILOGUE: THE ASCENDANCY
OF MANNERISM

(SOME EVENTS OF 1521)

669. ROSSO   *Madonna with Sts. John Baptist and Bartholomew*, Villamagna (near Volterra), Pieve

670. ROSSO *Deposition*, Volterra, Museum

488

671. ROSSO *Deposition* (detail)

672, 673. ROSSO *Deposition* (details)

490

674. PONTORMO *Design for Wall at Poggio a Cajano*, London, British Museum

675. PONTORMO *First Project for Lunette at Poggio*, Florence, Uffizi

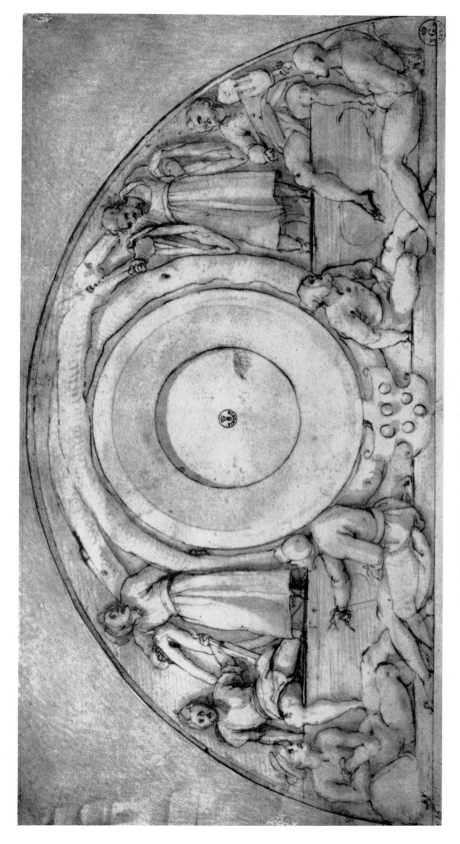

676. PONTORMO *Second Project for Lunette at Poggio*, Florence, Uffizi

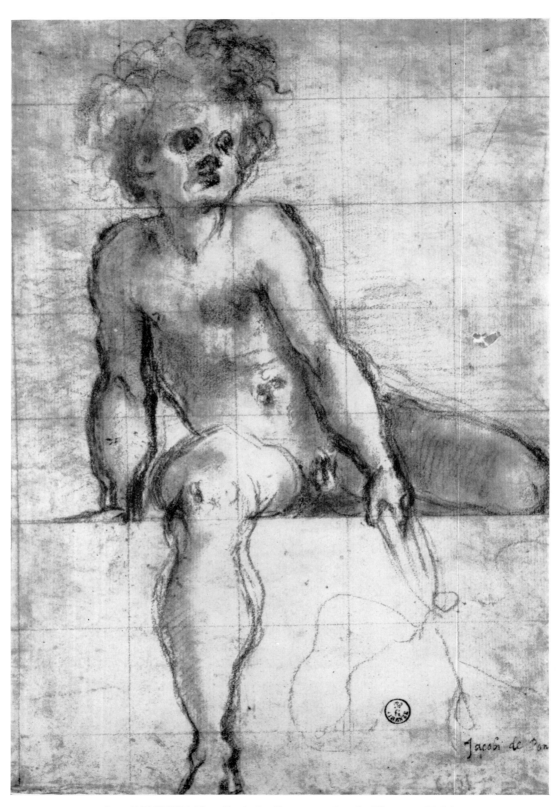

677. PONTORMO *Study for Lunette at Poggio*, Florence, Uffizi

678. PONTORMO *Vertumnus and Pomona*, Poggio a Cajano

495

679a. PONTORMO *Vertumnus and Pomona*, Poggio a Cajano

679b. PONTORMO *Vertumnus and Pomona*, Poggio a Cajano

680. PONTORMO *Vertumnus and Pomona* (detail)

681. GIOVANNI DA UDINE [and assistants] *Loggia*, Rome, Villa Madama

682. GIOVANNI DA UDINE [with Peruzzi] *Loggia* (central vault), Villa Madama

683, 684. GIOVANNI DA UDINE [with Peruzzi] *Loggia* (side vaults), Villa Madama

685, 686. PERUZZI *Loggia* (details), Rome, Villa Madama

687. GIOVANNI DA UDINE [with Perino] *Sala dei Pontefici*, Rome, Vatican

688. GIOVANNI DA UDINE [with Perino]   *Sala dei Pontefici* (detail)

689, 690. PERINO *Sala dei Pontefici* (details)

691. PERINO   *Sala dei Pontefici* (central panel of the vault)

692. GIULIO *Justice* (trial figure), Rome, Vatican, Sala di Costantino

693. GIULIO [and assistants]   *Sala di Costantino*, Rome, Vatican

694. GIULIO [and assistants]   *Sala di Costantino*, Rome, Vatican

695. GIULIO *Allocutio*, Sala di Costantino

696. GIULIO [and assistants] *The Battle of Constantine*, Sala di Costantino

697. GIULIO *St. Peter with Ecclesia and Aeternitas*, Sala di Costantino

698. GIULIO   *Leo X as Clement I with Moderatio and Comitas*, Sala di Costantino

699. GIULIO [and assistants]   *Battle of Constantine* (detail), Sala di Costantino

700. POLIDORO   *Basamento*, Sala di Costantino